KT-474-655

More Than My Job's Worth

John G. Muir

Christian Focus Publications

© 1993 John G. Muir
ISBN 1 85792 018 X

published by
Christian Focus Publications Ltd
Geanies House, Fearn, Ross-shire,
IV20 1TW, Scotland, Great Britain.

Cover design
by
Donna Macleod

Cover photograph
by
Zefa Picture Library
20 Conduit Place
London W2 1HZ

All rights reserved. No part of this publication may be repro-
duced, stored in a retrieval system, or transmitted, in any form
or by any means, electronic, mechanical, photocopying,
recording or otherwise, without the prior permission of
Christian Focus Publications.

All Bible quotations are from the New International Version,
published by Hodder and Stoughton, unless otherwise noted.

Printed and bound in Great Britain
by Cox & Wyman Ltd, Reading

Contents

FOREWORD

When Jesus called the 12 disciples, they gave up their everyday occupations to become key people in his ministry. All but one of them also turned out to be important leaders in the early Church.

At the same time thousands of others who were touched by Christ's message, remained in their jobs or stayed at home to bear witness to him in their daily lives. Among those encouraged to do so during his life were people like Nicodemus, Zacchaeus, Mary and Martha, to mention but a few. The New Testament gives us only an occasional glimpse into the lives of this army of believers before and after the resurrection but history records the impact they had on the world.

To-day also, only a few are called to full-time service. Are the rest only part-time Christians? What dilemmas do they face as they balance the demands of the secular and spiritual world? What challenges to their faith do they meet within their professions.

These are just a few of the questions that this book tries to answer through the testimonies of people from different walks of life and different church backgrounds, who have been willing to talk about some of the significant professional and spiritual milestones of their careers.

They talk about the 'grey' areas which we all encounter at some stage. But they give no slick answers, nor suggest easy ways to solve these dilemmas. Their accounts are interesting, at times humorous, and certainly testimony to the pivotal part that God plays in their lives.

I am grateful to each of them for allowing me to interview them and for their refreshing openness in expressing their opinions on secular and church life. I trust that those who read their stories will find them thought-provoking and challenging as they consider the issues of Christian living in today's world.

John G. Muir

Follow with reverent steps the great example
Of Him whose holy work was doing good;
So shall the wide earth seem our Father's temple,
Each loving life a psalm of gratitude.

John Greenleaf Whittier (1807-92)

1

Second Chance

The majestic setting of an ancient Highland castle seemed the ideal venue for the event. A steady stream of cars entered the magnificent tree-lined drive, as the limousines of royalty had done before them. Many of the rich and famous, responding to the personal invitation of the Countess, were already familiar with the place and felt at ease as they were ushered into the warm entrance hall. For the first-time visitor, looking around in wonder at the opulence of the historic building, there was perhaps an even greater sense of occasion.

A row of waiters in Highland dress stood to attention to welcome the guests to the mouth-watering buffet prepared before them. After a brief opening speech, the attendants moved speedily to ensure that everyone was served with food and drink. There was music and song to entertain and the Countess mingled with her guests to welcome them to her stately home. The whole event ran like clockwork. Everyone had a delightful evening, remarking at the excellence of the catering and the efficiency of the service.

As the chauffeurs arrived to take the guests home

that night, one person in particular was relieved that it had been such a successful occasion. Alastair Keddie, Community Service Organiser for a large local authority, was delighted that such a considerable sum had been raised to support various charities providing relief for troubled Romania. Just as importantly, he was pleased that the hand-picked caterers and waiters had performed so efficiently.

Although two of them were trained chefs, they were no ordinary employees, hired from a catering company for the evening. Rather, they were a group of people that, in other circumstances, the distinguished guests may have been reluctant to employ.

The young men who had served them so well on that memorable evening were convicted offenders, and the unusual charity event was part of their community service order. They counted it an honour to get inside the castle, but perhaps the final seal of success for them was the letter of thanks from the Romanian Ambassador and the privilege of taking their places in a group photograph of the Countess with her 'servants' for the day.

In the early eighties, when Alastair Keddie was given the task of taking over the leadership of the recently established pilot project, such an adventurous way to employ the offenders would have been unthinkable. They were, after all, criminals, people seen not to be trusted. Community service was once viewed, and still is by many, as an easy option, an attractive alternative to prison, by the public and some of the judiciary. The small number who were allowed by the courts to return to the community were given jobs that nobody else was likely to do.

Alastair recalled those early days. 'I felt very much that community service should not be seen as an easy option but more a second chance for selected offenders. Along with the opportunity to continue to live with their families, and perhaps find gainful employment, should be the chance to serve the community, as a means of restitution in a meaningful and dignified way. I have met so many people, whose lives have been destroyed by the prison system, for whom such a second chance was not an option when they were convicted.'

As organiser of one of the first four community service schemes in Scotland, Alastair has good credentials. With experience in a wide variety of social work, including case work in one of Scotland's largest prisons, he has learned to view the less fortunate in a more understanding way than most of us.

Much of this reflects the academic and practical training which he has been given as a professional but, above all, it is his Christian faith which he maintains has helped him to deal with the many people and situations he has encountered.

'I suppose the idea of community service being an opportunity for people to have a second chance comes from my own experience of life. I have reached the position that I am in today because God gave me a second chance in life. When I hear it proposed that, with some offenders, they should "lock them up and throw away the key", I think back to my own experience, not as a criminal certainly, but as an ordinary human being. The Christ of the Gospels encourages us to believe that even the worst offenders are still human beings to be reached. God is concerned for the whole man and all our needs are important to him.'

Although it is often easy to acknowledge guidance retrospectively, we are frequently unaware of what God is doing in our lives when it is all coming together in his plan at the time. This was very much the case with Alastair. He explained to me how he believed God had led him to where he is today in his career and in his faith. He spoke of difficult times in his childhood and the search for direction in employment in the middle years of life.

Born into a Christian home on the south side of Glasgow, just before the outbreak of the Second World War, he had a happy childhood. With his elder brother, he was introduced to the Bible and the Christian faith as far back as he can remember, attending church and Sunday School regularly. He got on well with many of his school friends but was a shy, retiring child in the classroom.

He loved sport, particularly swimming. One day, in the changing rooms at the local pool, he became aware that a swelling in his ankle he had noticed, seemed to be getting worse.

His parents took him to their doctor who was concerned enough to refer him to a specialist. To the dismay of his parents, tests showed that he had contracted a form of tuberculosis which affects the bones and joints. Now a rare disease, in those days TB was fairly common and could be infectious. Its association with poor diet attached a stigma to the condition even when this was clearly not the case.

His parents were devastated and the effect on Alastair

was no less severe. There followed a long period of hospitalisation and treatment after which his leg was in plaster and he could walk only with the aid of crutches. Even at the end of the treatment he was forced to wear a calliper on his leg. Although he had some teaching in hospital, he did not receive a regular secondary education. By the time he was 15, the normal school leaving age, he was so far behind that attending school would have been a relative waste of time.

'Not only did I not receive an adequate secondary education, but I also lost a great deal of my early teenage years - days when I should have been doing all the activities that other boys of my age could engage in. Looking back, I realise now the educational deficit I had when I started out to earn my living.'

He does not recall being embittered by the experience, no doubt due to the invaluable support of a Christian home and the encouragement of friends in his local church. While working with an engineering firm he tried to make up lost time by studying at evening classes and succeeded in gaining passes in a number of subjects. In the meantime, he attended church more out of habit than out of a sense of commitment.

'I was riding on the back of my parents' faith at that time, I suppose, but I did not have any sense of personal conviction. All and sundry thought I was a fine Christian. I was a conscientious young man, it appeared, and I was certainly not a rebellious teenager. After all, I had endured a lot, attended church regularly and even helped in the Sunday School, but I knew that it was just a weekend routine for me and little more.'

When the Billy Graham Crusade came to Glasgow

in 1955, along with many other young folk in his area, he attended pre-crusade rallies organised in a local church. The question of personal faith came up time and time again, the challenge culminating in the mass rally in the city centre.

'I had never attended such a great church event before. Still in my teens at the time, I was quite thrilled by the whole experience. Above all, I took on board the fact that I was relying on the faith of my parents and felt that one day it would not last for me.'

There was no blinding light, no startling emotional experience to overwhelm an impressionable teenager. For Alastair, it was simply a new beginning in his life, a chance to find Christ for himself. While his parents understood and supported him, looking back, he is aware that many of the folks in his local church couldn't understand what he was talking about as he seemed to be a fine Christian already.

'The expression 'born again' is used so widely, sometimes superficially, by many people, but that is really what it was for me. There was no outward dramatic change in what I did or said, but something had changed inside me.'

There then followed a period of growth in his personal and church life. His renewed inner faith found expression in outreach in the community, in prayer meetings, Bible studies and evangelistic services. Through the local church he was instrumental in establishing regular services in the nearby hospital, a much appreciated ministry which is still going on today. He also found a niche in work with young people and many were helped by his quiet and supportive ministry among them.

As he studied the Bible and was given the opportunity to help in church services he showed an interest in lay preaching and joined up with a team of young people in Glasgow to do evangelistic work in the city.

'We called ourselves The Ambassadors and visited churches of many denominations. I learned so much about the breadth of the Christian faith. I suppose my present belief that the gospel is not exclusive to one or other group of believers, stems from those early years.'

For the first time, he became aware that there were many people, young and old, who were 'beyond the pale', as far as some folk were concerned, and not just among the down and outs who frequented many such meetings in those days. It wasn't just a matter of singing and preaching to a captive audience. On more than one occasion, Alastair recalls how he felt so concerned about individuals, whose lives had been so much less fortunate than his own, that he tried to follow them up and help them, not only spiritually, but physically too: perhaps visiting a broken home, or talking into the night with a young person on the verge of suicide.

He enjoyed working with, and for, people and often wished that he could be in some full-time Christian work. This culminated in a desire to study for the ministry, but his limited formal secondary education proved to be a barrier. The chance to attend the Church of Scotland's St. Ninian's Centre in Perthshire to do a preparatory theology course, however, seemed an answer to prayer and he embarked on this excitedly.

His hopes were dashed when news reached him that his mother had been taken ill and he decided to return home after only one term of study. Sadly, she died a few months later and Alastair felt that he had to be at home with his ageing father. His mother had been the healthy one in the partnership and the whole family was stunned by her death. It seemed that a second chance to study and make up for lost years of education had slipped through his fingers.

'I could not understand what God was doing with my life. On each occasion I had tried to study, things had gone wrong. The ministry was no longer a possible option for me, but I lived with the idea of working full time for the church at some point in my life. In my prayers I could only ask, "Why?" and trust and believe.'

His work with young people continued unabated. As seaside mission organiser for the Scottish Evangelistic Council he planned and recruited young folk from all over Scotland to spend a week or two of their holidays working with local churches in far flung coastal parishes. Many of the young folk who joined the teams simply arrived at the mission venue, and valuable time had to be spent directing them how to share their faith with others.

Discussing this one winter evening with one of his co-organisers, Alastair had the idea to organise a series of pre-mission training and support conferences for team members. And so the SEC set up a Youth Training Department which, in association with other organisations involved in summer mission work, organised day and weekend training conferences for young people involved in Sunday Schools and youth work. These were not only highly successful, but also became the blueprint for many similar programmes continuing today.

Alastair found that, as well as providing an opportunity for young people to train for summer work ahead, the conferences allowed them to meet others, share their problems and have fellowship together.

'Many people I still have contact with today talk of those times and the encouragement it gave them to go on to do things they would not have previously considered.'

Alastair's desire to study further, to make up for lost time, continued. His daily employment in an electrical firm was little more than a means of earning money to support himself. Contact with students from the Bible Training Institute encouraged him to find out more about the courses they ran. He learned that his minimal education would not be a drawback if he wished to study a basic course. If accepted, he would be able to further his education and obtain a qualification in theology, one small step along the road to the ministry!

Unknown to him at the time, a close friend in church and mission work, was also considering applying to do the same course. After a long chat one evening over a meal, Alastair announced his intentions to him. The fact that he had been thinking along the same lines seemed to be confirmation of his plans. The main problem would be finance. While his friend would receive a grant to attend, Alastair learned that he was not eligible. Was this going to be yet another stumbling block for him? More than a little apprehensive, he filled in the application forms and waited.

As confirmation that he should attend, an anonymous gift to cover the first term's fees arrived one morning in the post and at the same time he was accepted for the course. Other gifts followed throughout the year.

The time of study at the Bible Training Institute was

a great blessing to him. The opportunity to extend his education was coupled with the invaluable experience of meeting Christians from all walks of life and from all corners of the world. In his second year as a day student, Alastair was elected president, reflecting the respect which many of his fellow students had for him. It was there also that he met a young nurse, Elizabeth, whom he would later marry.

Students from college are scattered far and wide today. Many are now missionaries abroad, many are in full time Christian work. That is what most people expected students to do. More difficult often was the decision that some had to make to simply return to everyday employment and benefit personally and devotionally from their studies. Alastair was one of a number who found themselves in that position.

For Alastair, it seemed that doors were still not opening to the ministry. A period of full time work at a Christian Centre in Lanarkshire, where he had wished to establish a pastoral ministry, did not fulfil his early vision.

Other invitations to full time work proved equally unfruitful. Now married and settled in a little flat in Central Scotland, his attention was drawn to a newspaper advertisement for a social worker with the Church of Scotland.

The job, working in a young women's hostel, with a daily parallel programme for homeless men in the city of Glasgow, appealed to Alastair and Elizabeth. Alastair applied and was interviewed for the post. It looked as if God had a plan for them in this work. But he was unsuccessful!

Disappointed, and more than a little disillusioned, he found part-time employment while Elizabeth continued nursing.

'Believe it or not, I was so convinced about the job I had applied for that, when I got a letter two weeks later from the Church of Scotland offering me the post as it was vacant again, I was not really taken aback.

'Working in the Tom Allan Centre was the first step in a career which finds me here today and another step towards that second chance I had prayed for. I had my mind set in one direction only, unaware that God had other plans along the way, other work that he wanted me to do.'

Then in his thirties, Alastair Keddie reckoned to have seen a lot of life around him, but working with the 'clients' at the Centre opened up a new dimension to him. There were girls, abused and abandoned; men, homeless and seemingly hopeless. The depth of deprivation and despair could have been utterly depressing were it not for the spiritual dimension which the hostel tried to foster in the work.

'The staff organised study groups, epilogues and group therapy classes; small, but important attempts to try to reach out to these people. Drink, rather than drugs, was the major problem then and we tried to support recovered alcoholics. The meetings were social, at times educational but, more often than not at their request, they turned to spiritual things. It was then that I became aware that our society had failed so many. It is easy to find fault with them but I often found myself saying, "There but for the grace of God...." '

A fair number of the clients found themselves in

prison, mainly for petty theft or vagrancy, but occasionally for more serious assaults and murder. Alastair learned then of some of the difficulties associated with prison life and some of the dilemmas he would encounter as a Christian in such work.

Despite the outreach and long discussions with those seeking something beyond their own wretched existence, there was sadness and disappointment. The occasional suicide, or the identification of a body at the morgue were poignant reminders, if they needed any, that their work was, at times, an uphill struggle.

'It is so easy to say that all we need to do is pray and preach. The dilemma for the social worker, even in Christian work, is that not all will be reached, but how do you know with whom you should try and try again? I recall my daughter Fiona's first birthday party attended by our family and friends. We had also invited some of the boys from the local epileptic hospital. I discovered that one of the girls, whom we had supported and prayed with on many occasions, had a birthday on the same day. She joined in the party and wanted to sing for us. I expected a rendering of *Happy Birthday* but instead, in a surprisingly attractive voice, she sang *Amazing Grace*. There was hardly a dry eye in the place! The next night we got a phone call to say that she had run off with one of the boys she had met at the party and was in trouble with the police in London.'

There were successful times too. It was always an encouragement for them to see families reunited, children settled in a stable home and men who were shining examples of God's help in their lives. A young voluntary worker, a convinced atheist, was so impressed with what she saw in the Centre that she became a Christian after many long discussions with Alastair and other members of staff.

On the occasional visit to prisons, he was concerned that so many people were caged up and out of touch with normal, everyday life. This was reinforced by his contact with a young man who regularly attended the Centre. Although talented in so many ways, he would repeatedly get into bad company and found himself in prison for drink-related offences.

Late one night Alastair was called out by the police to identify his body. While looking at the battered and lifeless figure on the mortuary slab, Alastair recalled the many evenings of counselling he had given him and wondered what he had achieved. He remembered how the young man shared with him the sense of despair that even the hardest criminals experienced when locked up and out of touch with society.

As he drove home in the early hours of the morning, he felt that he wanted to do something about it. But what and, above all, how? When he read of a social work post to undertake a pilot project to do research into prison life, he felt he should apply and was interviewed. He was unsuccessful.

'I was really certain that it was yet another step that God wanted me to take, although I did not know where it would all end. I was convinced that the job was for me, even when I did not get it! When I applied for another post with a well-known children's charity, I knew that it was wrong, even when I was offered the post. The fact that we could not find accommodation to enable me to take up the position, confirmed my reservations.'

Nine months later, a phone call offered him the job in the prison. History had repeated itself, or to put it more spiritually, God was working to plan. A twist to the story is that, no sooner had he been appointed, when he was offered a newly built three-bedroomed bungalow by the children's charity if he would go and work for them.

Moving from a place where he could pray with the staff and residents at the start of every day, to a regimented institution where the inmates slopped out every morning, was a sharp contrast, to say the least. As a government employee, he realised also that his faith in action would have to become less overt.

'Those early days were hard, but I learned so much that would enable me to help others in later years. I learned that the worst thing for a prisoner was not confinement - you can be confined to bed at home or in a hospital - but the loss of personal identity. In prison, he has no rank, no title, no right to vote or to contact home when he wishes, no choice of clothing or freedom to wash when he pleases. The project I was involved in was set up to look into the total effect that these conditions had on the inmates.'

Placed initially in a hall for short-term prisoners, he was given permission to be alone with them to allow privacy and gain their confidence. This was contrary to normal practice and caused some friction, at first, with the prison officers who felt that their authority was being undermined.

'I believed that it was important to reach out to the men where they were. I would shake hands with them, a gesture I learned many of them appreciated. In doing this to a prisoner I was acknowledging him as a person. Physical contact, no matter how minor, was generally frowned upon. We also addressed each other by our surnames. I stopped them calling me "sir".

'I had equal rights with the prison chaplain, but I knew that I was not there to preach to them but to talk to them, to help them liaise with the community and the world outside. In some small way the aim was to keep them part of the same society that had punished them.'

There were opportunities to speak to them about Christian things, if they raised it or if the moment seemed right. What was important was that Alastair tried to show that they mattered as human beings.

'When asked from time to time to find out about a sick relative, a prisoner might say, "If you don't have time, it doesn't matter." I would reply that it did matter and would do my best to get a message to them. A message which I once left for a prisoner whose child was sick was not passed on by an officer, who had little respect for what I was trying to do with the inmates. On learning of this I took it up with the Principal Officer, pointing out that my authority and ability to do my job as a social worker were being undermined. I wanted the men to believe that even minor concerns did matter.'

I put it to Alastair that some might say that the basic restriction on communicating the gospel directly called the work into question for a Christian in that situation.

'I did not know when I took on the job what restrictions there would be but, on occasion, I was able to go back in the evening in my own time to speak to them. Also on a day-to-day basis, I was able to foster trust and integrity, keep my word and be fair, all qualities alien to most prisoners. I did not go in as a super-Christian able to solve all their problems. I felt that Christ would sit with them too, would speak to them, care for them and treat them like human beings. We read in the Bible, "I was imprisoned and you visited me".'

Part of the research was to learn why inmates commit further offences while in prison, which has its own court system. His work allowed him to visit them once they had been sentenced. One fellow had been charged with failing to concentrate properly at his work and being sullen and aggressive. He said little before or after he had been sentenced.

'I learned that he had received a letter that morning telling him that his uncle had died. Not too drastic you may think, but this man had been like a father to him and he was heartbroken. This was the only way he knew to express his grief. But sentence had been passed and there was no appeal.

'Another man attempted suicide. The officers and I found him hanging in his cell. He was taken before the governor and punished by being put into solitary confinement, which shocked me to the core. When I went in to see him he was clad only in his underwear and lying on the cell floor, alone and in utter despair. He shared his thoughts with me and I learned that he had heard on the prison grapevine that his wife had gone off with another man. That was the last straw, as far as he was concerned. Believe it or not, their marriage and a wife waiting for them outside is what keeps many of them going. Despite all this, there was no appeal.

'I despair at times and, yes, feel very angry when I learn of such cases. Even if we keep reminding ourselves that these people have committed crimes against society, we gain nothing by turning a blind eye to alleged maltreatment and injustice.

'Society as a whole is reluctant to support penal reform and improvements in prison conditions, particularly when resources are scarce. What is more important, new schools or new prisons? In some ways, this is the biggest dilemma for me as a Christian working with people convicted of crimes. In prison there is rarely a second chance. An increasing number of prisoners are readmitted and at enormous cost to society. I believe that Christians must be made more aware of this and be led to consider what alternatives to prison there might be for some individuals. And for those for whom prison is the only option, what can we do to break into the never ending and costly cycle of re-offending?

'Although not so active in those days, the Prison Christian Fellowship now does a great job in many of our jails. I have learned that many Christians are unfamiliar with the fine work they do.'

Alastair wanted his voice to be heard, to have some influence, as a social worker as much as a Christian, but opportunities for promotion within the system were hindered by his lack of formal qualifications.

When a college place became available for further study, he applied and was unsuccessful. Yet again, he was surprised by the outcome because he felt that it was right for him. Following the already familiar pattern of events in his life (now seeming more and more like Divine guidance!) he was offered a place a few weeks later, just as the course was commencing.

It was to prove an interesting, yet difficult, time for

them. In addition to Fiona, they now had Gordon and Stuart, twin boys born just before they left Glasgow. It was not easy to maintain a home and care for a family on such a reduced income but, fortuitously, Elizabeth secured a part-time nursing post.

Adjusting to student life was a particular challenge but he enjoyed the opportunity to study and take one more step forward in the second chance to catch up on his education. His experience was broadened through placements including a children's home, a social work office and a hospital.

Conscious of God's guidance in their lives to date, Alastair and Elizabeth trusted that a post would become available after qualifying, as he had to give up the appointment in the prison to take up the course. They were not to be disappointed, or even turned down on the first application this time. In contrast, the local area manager of the Social Work Department called at their home one evening to offer Alastair a job!

'It was most unusual. In fact, I often think of the gentleman appearing that evening, like an angel in disguise, just when we did not know where to go next.'

He was immediately appointed to the local Social Work Department where he had a case load which included multi-problem families, children at risk and in care, the elderly and, of particular interest to him, prisoners on parole.

When there was a national decision to explore the idea of community service as an alternative to custodial sentences, Alastair found himself in the right place at the right time and with the background and training to take a leading position in the newly established programme.

'The whole ethos of community service seemed to reflect so much of what I had wished to see developing in the system that I could only look back in amazement at how God had seen fit to direct and allow me to be trained to be where I am now. I certainly could not have planned my career with this eventuality in mind.'

Alastair was appointed to lead one of the programmes which was now up and running. Available at first to a very restricted number of offenders, reflecting the hesitation of many within the legal system, he was instrumental in encouraging a much wider application of the orders. Then there were only two officers under his charge, but today there are more than thirty of a staff in post in his area. Viewed initially as a soft alternative to prison, some offenders responded readily to the opportunity.

'I was aware of the reluctance of the courts to see this as a form of punishment but, convinced of the worth of the approach, I made it my job to try to ensure that it would achieve credibility. One important point I stressed with offenders was that, if community service was accepted as an alternative to prison, they had to realise that prison would be an alternative to community service.

'The problem is that community service can seem to go on for months on end while 30 days in prison is over in no time for the habitual offender for whom gaol is familiar. I have been verbally abused by an offender who claimed he was being "exploited" by being made to work without pay.

'The difference would be their freedom and, for many of them, the "second chance" I keep referring to. The great advantage, as I see it, is that those who have committed crimes against society can make restitution to that same group of people by doing meaningful tasks.'

Community service orders can extend from 40 to 240 hours, depending on the nature of the offence, and it was not easy at first for Alastair and his team to identify work acceptable to the community and to the unemployed, who tended to see them as low priced competitors for available work. It is a sad reflection on the employment situation today that, for some of the young people involved in community service, it is the first job they ever have.

Projects rarely include such newsworthy events as charity buffets for the well-to-do, described in the introduction, but Alastair feels strongly that good publicity like this can only benefit the self esteem of the offenders. Most of the time they are tidying gardens, painting, cleaning beaches or making forest walks, to give but a few examples of the many worthwhile things they have been asked to do. Many elderly people and single parents are greatly helped by the army of some 300 offenders who do work in the community, organised by Alastair's team.

Another notable innovation is a project with blind children. Supervised offenders look after groups of blind children, taking them swimming, walking, and on visits to places of interest. In this way their hard-pressed parents and other carers are given some respite for a few days per month, during holiday periods. It was highly acclaimed in the country because it was caring on a one to one basis rather than a purely physical activity. Indeed, so successful and innovative have many of the projects been, that a video of some of the work in

Alastair's area has been used for training courses with other authorities.

'I believe that building the self-esteem of an individual is a step towards his reformation. Of course, I believe that only the gospel of Christ will have the ultimate effect of changing them but, I have come to understand that often the two must go together. The gospel restores self-respect because Jesus thought the person valuable enough to die for. So often in the Bible we see how Jesus showed individuals that they were important to him, that their lives mattered - take Zacchaeus, for example - and then he spoke of eternal things.'

Alastair has come under fire from Christians who have felt that he has got the order for action wrong, or who feel that he is denying society the opportunity to mete out effective deterrents. Others feel strongly that he should be more overt with his beliefs when dealing with the offenders. But he believes that honesty, integrity and fairness are the most important initial steps and clearly acceptable to his employers.

Staff and others have come to learn that Alastair Keddie is fair, doesn't lose his temper, doesn't swear and perhaps is more tolerant than many others of misdemeanours. But he stresses greatly that he never wishes to be considered a 'soft touch'. It is necessary therefore on occasion to discipline staff and offenders who have abused their position by taking advantage of the work they are asked to do in the community.

'I know of Christians in different professions who have made the job difficult by seeing their charges, first and foremost, as souls to be *won* and it has been hard for me to inhibit their zeal. I feel that I would be abusing my position if I effectively rammed the gospel down the throats of the offenders.'

But Alastair does not neglect to take the opportunity to testify to his faith when he deems it appropriate. When a young man on community service, who appeared to be making headway in his life, crashed a stolen car, he was seriously injured and in a coma when admitted to hospital. Several evenings a week, in his own time, he visited the youth to read and pray with him.

There are many people today who are undoubtedly grateful for the 'second chance' which Alastair Keddie offered, or arranged to be provided for them. Much of his work latterly has been under conditions of strict confidentiality and names are unlikely ever to be revealed. Tracing his educational progress and the path of secular and Christian work along which he has very obviously been directed, it is clear that the offer of support and the hand of friendship stretched out to so many, has reflected his keen sense of gratitude for the 'second chance' which he believes God gave him.

Footnote: At the time of publication, Alastair took up the offer of early retirement from his post following a reorganisation of the service. He is now studying for the ministry - another step forward in that 'second chance'.

2
Guiding Principles

You could have knocked him down with a feather. John* and Melanie* couldn't help but notice that he was stunned by what they had told him. Even as they spoke, the Rev Tom Jones* shook his head in disbelief, his eyelids flickering nervously.

He had known them since they were children in the Sunday School, had officiated at their wedding and had baptised their two lovely daughters. He couldn't think of a more suited couple; committed Christians and actively involved in the church. What had happened to them? Why had he not been aware that something might be wrong?

All sorts of memories and concerns flashed through his mind as he sat in their home that evening. He had called to talk about plans for the new session with the Youth Group but they had confided their story to him and announced that they may be leaving the area - separately.

'So you see Tom, we feel we just don't love each other any more,' John concluded.

'But what's the problem? Can we talk more about it

(* not their real names)

and, more importantly, can I help in any way?' Tom Jones asked, after what seemed an age of silent disbelief.

'There's just about everything wrong with our marriage and we're not really living together as a couple any more,' Melanie added, her eyes filling with tears.

Further questions led to embarrassed looks between them until Melanie left the room when, conveniently, one of the children could be heard crying upstairs.

'Look John,' urged Tom when he was alone with him, 'I admit that I'm still a bit shell-shocked, but maybe I'm not the person you should be telling all this to. I know someone who can help; someone who is a Christian and who is also a trained counsellor in these matters. Would you like me to give her a call and make an appointment for you both to meet her?'

As far as the young couple were concerned, anything was worth a try if their marriage was to be rescued. At the first meeting with Meg Duncan, the counsellor referred to by their minister, they explained that they argued constantly and that the bickering and frustration was beginning to affect their children.

Further discussion led to John's admitting that he had felt left out, if not rejected, when the children appeared. All Melanie's energy was being expended on them and in keeping the home tidy and organised. For her part, Melanie complained that John was always out of the house, either working overtime or in church activities. He was never around to help her in the house or share in caring for the children and rarely ever showed her any affection. In short, she felt that he was taking her totally for granted.

The resentment and anger built up over the years

until they only communicated in a way that put each other down and had moved to a position where conversations were point scoring feuds. Love-making had ceased some time ago as he felt frustrated and rejected at her repeated excuses.

Counselling began by making them aware of what their communication patterns had done to each other's self-esteem. Then they looked very hard and long at how their negative patterns of communication and inability to resolve any conflict had resulted in their failing to achieve what they most wanted - a loving, secure, intimate relationship.

Meg explained further, 'This was done in the counselling room by my refusing to act as referee and by my constantly feeding back to them the recurring patterns and challenging them to acknowledge their feelings. I asked them whether they felt they had any hope for their relationship and gave them responsibility to make a commitment to work at improving it. Eventually they were able to begin to be honest with each other.'

Melanie and John were from different backgrounds. She came from a family who were openly affectionate and showed their feelings. John had a very distant father who had high expectations of his achievements and a mother who did not show her feelings. To compound this, his mother made it clear that she felt that to do so was childish.

'Interestingly, it emerged,' Meg continued, 'that John seemed to have put the earthly characteristics of his father on to his heavenly Father and viewed God as distant and judgmental. He was constantly trying to please him and gain acceptance.

'As they learned slowly to risk being positive - difficult when you are vulnerable and afraid of rejection - they looked also at the power of God's healing love, the intimacy of a Saviour who loved his bride so much as to give his life for her. They saw God's plan for a husband and wife to submit to each other and to serve one another, for a husband to sacrificially love his wife and for a wife to do all she could to respect and build up her husband's esteem.'

At one point, when Melanie was distressed and weeping, Meg asked John what he felt like doing when he saw her unhappiness. He replied that previously he had always wanted to run away but now he felt that he wanted to touch and comfort her. However, he was afraid that she would reject him, yet again. When she immediately responded by telling him that she wanted his affection more than anything, the barriers began to break down.

'Eventually they worked through a programme which involved their returning to their "courtship days", re-establishing touch and building up their sexual intimacy while communication and trust were being established.

'They began to pray together also, not trying to manipulate each other but being real before God and each other, confessing their inadequacies, longings and needs. This young couple are doing well now and are working hard at being faithful to love, accept and value each other.'

John and Melanie are one of many couples who have turned to Meg Duncan for help. Not surprising, perhaps, in an age when one in three marriages break down within a short time of the exchange of rings. Such statistics reflect the common knowledge that more and more couples seem less committed to their marriage than their grandparents might have been. Living together before marriage, so called 'open' relationships, seem to be the order of the day, brazenly endorsed by the media in general and films and soap operas in particular.

But it is particularly disturbing that Christian couples, committed to remember the vows they took under God before the altar, 'until death...', seem prey to the problems which can beset relationships not sealed with such a promise.

Thirty years ago, Meg Duncan was more concerned about troublesome molars than troubled marriages and, if anyone had suggested to her then that in the 1990s she would be counselling couples with marital difficulties, she might have laughed in disbelief. Her training in dentistry did not include a consideration of the complexities of human relationships but, as she revealed her story to me, the reasons for that quantum leap to a vastly different profession, gradually became clear. Her home background, her later training and, certainly, her Christian commitment, all played a part in leading her to the work she is called to do at present.

The home of her early childhood was a happy one and she remembers many enjoyable times together as a family. Although her parents were not professing Christians they sent Meg to Sunday School along with her brother and sister.

It came as a considerable shock to her, therefore, at the age of seven, to learn that her father had a major drink problem; it was a tribute to her mother that she had been protected from the knowledge for so long. But the secret was maintained for many years after that, despite the active social life of the family and the steady stream of visitors welcomed to their home.

'Even as I speak, I hesitate to reveal it, but I now realise that the story I have to tell about my present involvement in counselling has been influenced by these memories and the tensions which existed in my parents' relationship.'

Not unnaturally, she grew up with a lot of confused messages swirling around in her head during these formative years. As if that were not enough for an impressionable youngster to cope with, when she was nine years old she had a short spell of scarlet fever, followed later by a form of rheumatism which confined her to bed for the best part of a year.

A home tutor was assigned to her and, although a poor substitute for the normal educational and social interactions of the classroom, she was able to continue with her schooling. She did recover sufficiently to join her friends at the local school but, during her teenage years there were occasional relapses, confining her to bed for up to six months at a time. Mercifully, she was well enough to go to university but, in her later years, the trouble would return from time to time.

When confined to bed she often read and listened to the radio to relieve the boredom of staring at bedroom walls day in and day out. During one of these bad spells when she was a teenager, Meg remembers tuning into gospel radio stations broadcasting the Christian message. With the volume turned down, so as not to disturb the rest of the household in the dead of night, she listened intently to what those far away preachers had to say. Their message had a great impact on her.

'As I lay in bed during these bouts, I despaired at times and felt that there had to be something more to life than what I was experiencing. I got to know about the Scripture Union in my secondary school and began to attend to find out more about the things I had heard on the radio. I reached a stage when I challenged God to show me that he really did exist. When I got a hold of a Bible, I started to read it regularly and was soon totally caught up in the uniqueness of Jesus and the revelation of God through him.'

In the small group of Christians which met at school, she asked all the awkward questions that a searching teenager might ask. When one of her friends, whom she knew to be a bit of a rebel at school, 'got religion' during the Billy Graham Crusade in the 1950s she was amazed at the transformation in her life.

'I wanted what she had and I switched from challenging God to asking him to show me how I could change too. It was not at any crusade, however, that the whole thing came together for me, but at a service in the church I had begun to attend. One morning the words of the sermon came home to me like a bullet. *Either Jesus is God's Son or he was mad or he was a liar*. I knew that I had to believe in Jesus and trust him as my Saviour there and then, on my own, without any further prompting.'

What she had heard on the radio in the solitude of her own room and the fruit of the discussions she had had with her friends at school, all came together as she listened to the sermon that morning. She knew that something had happened to her, that a change had taken place in her life, but her family's reaction was to tell her that she was just 'going through a phase' and would soon grow out of it. But she grew into it, not out of it and, as she read the Bible and heard the Word of God preached, her faith became stronger.

In her early teens, her ambition was to become a doctor. The reality of her chosen career dawned on her forcefully when she witnessed two fatal accidents. Fearing that she would have difficulty coping with the distress and pain of such emergencies, she decided that dentistry would be an interesting alternative.

'I was not so spiritually aware then as to think of God guiding me in one direction or another but, in retrospect, I realise that he clearly was. If I had studied medicine then I don't feel that God could have led me into counselling in the future.

'Thinking back to my very first year, I recall going into the student hostel, feeling lonely and more than a little apprehensive. The first person I met shook my hand and welcomed me warmly. I later learned that she was a Christian and she was instrumental in introducing me to the Christian Union where I met others who gave me fellowship during these days.'

It was there also that she met Hugh, a fellow student, who would become her husband. Hugh was from a Christian background and, through his family, she experienced for the first time the welcome and warmth which a Christian home can offer.

After six years of study, she qualified, moved to London with her husband and joined a dental practice there. When she became pregnant she gave up dentistry and, shortly after that, moved again when her husband set up business in another part of the country. With four daughters, each a couple of years apart in age, motherhood replaced dentistry as her full-time occupation. She had time, however, to become involved in church activities in the little town where they settled down to bring up their family.

'Things were not too exciting, to say the least, in our church in those days, but there was a lively group who met together to pray and have fellowship. The work in the church grew and was a great support to many people in the town and surrounding area.'

Their house became home from home to many young people who appreciated the fellowship the family offered them. It was at this time that Meg began to realise that she wanted to reach out to people, many of whose lives seemed to be in turmoil. A number of them had problems but lived a lie when in the public eye, just as the family of her childhood had done all those years ago.

When the family grew up, she could easily have returned to dentistry but, from the short time she had spent in practice, she knew that she would rarely have the chance to meet and talk to people on other than a superficial basis in that profession. Meeting and reaching out to help people in their lives was something she felt she wanted to do more regularly than being in a practice would allow her.

'I have the highest regard for dentistry of course, and the excellence of the profession is not in question, but I felt that I, personally, would not be completely fulfilled as a Christian in what I wanted to do, if I returned at that time.'

On holiday one summer in the early 70s, Meg and

her husband became friendly with someone whom they learned was a marriage guidance counsellor. Through her they got to know about the work of the movement. Thinking back to the challenges in her own parents' marriage and in the relationships of many of the people she had met through church work, she considered becoming a counsellor.

'I had a happy marriage and felt that there may be some way that I could help others to find happiness too. What was not clear in my mind at that time was how things would develop when I had to counsel others who were not Christians. This was, in fact, to become a major dilemma for me as I will talk about later.'

After her selection for training as a counsellor she was challenged over the training period of two years to think of herself, her motives for choosing this profession, her attitudes and the messages she carried over from her childhood. She learned about the psychology of human development, about relationship patterns and about negative and positive communication. She also began to have an understanding about alcohol, emotional and sexual abuse and sexual problems.

'I began to realise that almost everybody who was not living as God intended them to live, when we really got under the surface of their relationships, yearned for the "real thing". God created us to be truly fulfilled only as we live according to his will and design. For example, many talked about "open marriages" and the great freedom to have affairs. Others claimed to see no necessity for marriage at all and saw chastity as an outmoded virtue. Some maintained that their homosexuality was simply an alternative and acceptable way of living and wished advice on how to overcome the problems they had to face.

'But in my conversations with them I saw that, where they confessed to experience no guilt, underneath it all many were incredibly guilty about how they were living. More often than not, the majority longed for a normal, more socially acceptable, relationship. I shouldn't have been surprised about this because I believe that God has created us to want those things. Jesus said, "At the beginning of creation God made them male and female. For this reason a man will leave his father and mother and be united to his wife and the two will become one flesh. So they are no longer two, but one" (Mark 10:6-8).'

The marriage guidance system is client-centred. Counsellors work with the clients' goals in mind and use the 'here and now' of their relationship with them. Meg learned so much from the training which took this philosophy into account and, although it is clearly secular in its basis, she has found it to be an excellent way of working with all those whom she counsels at present. It deals also with the importance and worth of the individual and the whole issue of personality development.

'I still feel it is an appropriate way of working. There can be a tendency in Christian counselling to spiritualise everything which allows people to avoid their responsibility for behaving in certain ways and to escape from the reality of the situation. Problems, even within Christian marriages, are often not spiritual but emotional and physical at the root of the matter.'

Notwithstanding the great respect she has for the

movement, Meg became acutely aware that so many of the solutions she had to offer couples were based on Christian principles. A two-tier practice seemed to be developing, as Christian couples came and returned to her while she continued to counsel others on a secular basis.

'When some Christians came to me as a secular counsellor, depending on their needs, I would not always reveal my own beliefs. Some, for their part, were embarrassed when they realised that I was a Christian.'

Meg progressed in the organisation and gained considerable experience. She was held in high regard by the leadership and clients alike and was given the opportunity to become a tutor, to train and supervise others. There was a little more freedom for her to express her Christian views, but the dilemma of her situation came to a head when one of the counsellors in training turned out to be a practising Buddhist. Meg challenged her one day about what she would do about her desire to proselytise for the Buddhist faith with her clients.

'It occurred to me, even as I waited for an answer, that I might also plead guilty to proselytising for the Christian faith under cover of the movement and here was I unhappy that someone else should do the same with another religion! I knew that it was right for me to do so but I still felt restricted on occasion and could not give them what I saw as the biblical solution to their problem. I had a real dilemma which I suddenly realised I had to meet head on.

'Much of what I was doing was *relationship counselling* and I had to deal with people whose lifestyle and beliefs were so alien from my own. The marriage guidance movement was dealing with the reality of two or three marriages in the course of people's lives, with living together, adultery and homosexuality viewed as normal practices. I had to ask myself, "What am I doing here and where am I going?"

'As a Christian, I felt that I could pray for wisdom in my counselling, be loving and compassionate as only one who knows the reality of God's love can be. But I very often wanted to offer more, especially when people felt that their lives were hopeless, empty and meaningless.'

At that time she was selected to train as a psychosexual counsellor and, in the discussion groups, she found at times that she was at variance with the recommendations and advice being offered. She was particularly concerned about the counselling recommended for homosexuality and the moral dilemma of hormonal and surgical treatment for people who wished to change their sex.

'They thought I was a Roman Catholic at first but I had to tell them that I was simply a practising Christian who had problems with some of their ideas. I learned so much from this course about the treatment of basic sexual problems which can arise in any marriage that it has been a great help to me in the work I now do.'

As her practice grew with more and more Christian clients, there were increased opportunities to talk about how God's word had very practical things to say about relationships, and opportunities to share his love, forgiveness and healing.

She was particularly concerned when a well known

Christian personality came to her to 'confess' his homosexuality and expressed his wish to 'come out', leave his wife and live a gay life style. When she challenged him to think deeper and to look at God's will for him, he was embarrassed and taken aback to discover that she was a Christian. Nevertheless, he continued to see her and discuss his problem with her, but did not alter his stance. Her actions now, not only her beliefs, seemed to be at odds with the work she was doing. Meg stresses, however, that she would not go so far as to say that it is impossible for any Christian to work within Marriage Guidance, probably better known as Relate in some parts of the country.

'It is just that I felt that I could not work exclusively with them from that time onwards. I have the utmost admiration and respect for the excellent work they do. So many have found support and help that I could not but acknowledge their many achievements and, more particularly in my case, the excellence of their training and basic philosophy, which recognises the worth of the individual.'

To break from this work after ten years of counselling was not easy for her. This had been her life, she had enjoyed it and had to face up to the fact that she did not know where to go next. The service was sorry to loose her as they valued her work and appreciated her sincerity, but they also accepted the reasons for her decision to leave.

'I remember praying at that time and being afraid that God would ask me to get involved in public speaking at some point. I had been receiving invitations to speak about counselling and had always chickened out. At the same time, however, I knew that there was a need for Christians to speak out about God's principles, his patterns and the things that the Bible had to say about human sexuality, relationships within marriage and the rearing of children.'

She now believes that God has a sense of humour because, the very thing she dreaded doing, has become an important aspect of her ministry. The excuse she had often made to God in the past was that the rheumatic problem she once had, raised its head whenever she was under stress of any kind. To her utter amazement and that of her doctor, she found that the condition did not return! Her GP informed her that, for some strange reason, it was quiescent and she could now lead a more normal life. As more and more invitations to speak came in, she did get the strength to address larger and larger groups of people about her work and the principles she believes in.

'I believe God has shown me the importance of communication between people. I often encourage them to share together and think about the issue of communication in their family life. I ask them to look at their commitment to their family. Are they being fulfilled with their children and with their partners? How central to them are the principles laid down in the Bible? "Fix these words of mine in your hearts and minds ... Teach them to your children, talking about them when you sit at home and when you walk along the road" (Deut. 11:18-19).'

But invitations to speak to groups around the country were only one of many aspects of the work she felt she should be doing. She had hoped that her years of experience and training would be put to use in a more specific role as a counsellor in a Christian context.

It was a real answer to prayer, as far as she was concerned, when the health centre, with whom she had worked as a marriage counsellor, asked her to continue working with them on a voluntary basis with private clients on occasion. They indicated to her that they valued the work she was doing and particularly appreciated her experience in psycho-sexual medicine. She felt that this was a clear vindication of the path of training she had chosen to pursue, difficult though it was at the time to come to terms with it as a Christian.

'They told me that, if I was willing to see their patients, I was free to use the accommodation to speak to my own clients. Many people come to see me, Christian and non-Christian; those with marital problems or breakdowns through bereavement, health, abuse or whatever. As far as those patients who are referred to me from the practice are concerned, it is not my role to lead them to Christ, but I have freedom, nevertheless, to speak to them about spiritual things if I feel it to be appropriate in the circumstances. Complete confidentiality is maintained and I do not pass on information automatically to others in the centre.'

The non-directive approach which she takes with her clients is not provocatively evangelical but, as her clients become aware of themselves and their own particular needs, they are frequently open to biblical principles in the guidance she offers. In her previous position she did not have the freedom to do this.

'It is more that I promote the Christian ethic in the approach to marital problems, than overtly or aggressively preach the gospel to them. A large proportion of my work is to do with emotional and physical difficulties which do not have a spiritual solution, just as it might be for someone who speaks to their doctor about some medical condition they may have. But most of my clients now are from a Christian background and the counselling can frequently allude to spiritual things.'

Meg feels saddened by the fact that there is no forum within many churches for young people to discuss their relationships and sexuality in a biblical context, nor is there an opportunity for young couples to have counselling on any relationship problems they may have. She has found that, too often, couples enter marriage on the basis of their Christian faith alone and have not learned what it means to share and communicate with each other on a physical and emotional plane. Physical attraction to each other, she maintains, is a basic component of a happy marriage, and she does not simply mean 'good looks'!

Perhaps they were given a book by an embarrassed parent or have picked up a few odds and ends of information at school or college, but problems inevitably arise when knowledge is only biologically based. She spoke of the need for children and adolescents to be aware of their parents' relationship and to see them being affectionate with each other.

'When children see their parents talking and sharing things together, kissing and cuddling, or are touched affectionately by them, they are learning the basic principles of relating and communicating physically with the opposite sex. Sadly, this whole experience has been sullied by the much reported abuse of children by adults. Yet physical contact and verbal communication are among the essential elements of a healthy, close relationship.

'Down through the ages, the church, more often than not, has viewed sex as a necessary evil for the continuation of the species. Yet this is not biblical. In fact, God thought of sex first! Time and time again throughout the Scriptures, and very specifically within Song of Solomon, we see the value which God puts on the purity of the relationship between husband and wife. That the church is described as his bride, only serves to underline his thoughts on the matter.

'We like to think that we are more enlightened today, but many couples who come to me have problems because they have difficulty accepting that all aspects of their relationship play a part in the bonding which God intended them to experience. *Cleaving*, described in the Bible, is essential and yet it does not just happen. Couples have to work at it. Sadly, the church tends to avoid the topic, openly at least, and few vicars, ministers or elders are comfortable in preparing young people for marriage or discussing any marital problems which may arise later on.'

One of the most common emotions she encounters in couples is resentment which has built up gradually over the years of their relationship. One may resent not having physical contact; the other may resent the lack of time to be together, to touch, listen and share. Couples need to learn how to communicate and work through their 'ouch' areas before they build up into anger and malice. The craving for intimacy, emotionally and physically, is a basic human need, she underlines, and

God has created us with bodies which can express that within marriage.

'It is often said that women require intimacy, whereas men grow out of that when they are no longer children and they are "stronger". This is most definitely not the case. The failure of men to admit this need, or of their wives to recognise it in a relationship, is the root of many a problem with couples who come to me.'

Meg has come to realise also that some Christians feel that they must always be on a high spiritual plane and cannot come to terms with any weaknesses or failings in their relationships. The poor self-esteem which many individuals have is often the basis of the breakdown.

'Much of my work with couples initially is aimed at increasing the value they place on themselves. The Bible says that we must love others as we love ourselves. It follows, therefore, that we must have a good self-esteem before we can fully love and relate to our partners.'

Her ministry is as much about making churches aware of those needs as it is about helping couples. The fact that more and more ministers are referring members of their congregation to her reflects the increasing value which they place on her work. Sadly also, the strains of marriage in the manse are only too common and she has been able to help many a couple cope with the stress of relationships caused by being in the ministry.

'It is possible for people in Christian work, and that includes the clergy, to be so involved in reaching out to others that they neglect their own relationships and family life. This is something which congregations and leaders must become more aware of.'

Although she now has more freedom to express her beliefs when counselling, Meg is also aware that many challenges and dilemmas remain even when dealing with Christian clients. So much is clear in Scripture about the issues of separation and divorce but, when she encounters hurt, violence and severe abuse in a relationship, it is often very hard to find biblical solutions to the problem.

'I know that God can do the impossible but, sadly, I still know of couples who, unknown to their friends and relatives, live in an atmosphere of incredible cruelty behind smiling "Christian" masks. There seems no alternative but for me to agree that separation is the only immediate solution.'

Ever conscious that such advice may seem to be at odds with the biblical view of marriage, and that it may fuel gossip among those who are already sceptical about the work she is doing, she is also aware that the health and safety of a wife and children may be at risk in certain circumstances. She would stress, however, that the love of Christ can lead to reconciliation with some couples when the abuser as well as the abused have been counselled and helped by God.

Healing, however, can be a lengthy and heart-searching process. In some parts of the country there are Christian hostels, 'safe' places for those who have been abused to be counselled.

'It is easy to say it is wrong for a Christian couple to split up - and I still believe that God can intervene even in extreme cases - but I could tell you of situations where life-threatening violence can only be avoided by separation. It cannot be part of God's plan to allow the infliction of pain and suffering to continue unabated, if reconciliation seems impossible in the short term. This is an increasingly frequent dilemma which troubles me greatly.'

She shares this dilemma with other Christian professionals, including doctors, health visitors and solicitors whose advice has been sought in harrowing circumstances. Sadly, it is an area of conflict too often avoided by the church, whose members may be only too quick to say 'tut, tut' if a marriage breaks down and criticise advice given by counsellors such as Meg.

Many excellent books have been written for families and young people who seek guidance on the biblical view of courtship, marriage and the family. Meg commends many of these publications for she believes that advice and guidance, based on Christian principles, must be given before marriage so that young couples are aware of the limits which they should set in their relationship. Mutual respect, and an understanding of the biblical roles of husband and wife, do not automatically occur after the vows have been taken.

'Many couples I have spoken to confess now to being aware that, even before their marriage, all was not right between them. Somehow, they felt that it was alright to go as far as they wished sexually when they were courting, even if they had only recently met. Perhaps they thought that things would change once they were living together as man and wife; anything they had done wrong, or any differences they had between them, would be resolved once they were married.

'Often what they need to do first of all is to ask for God's forgiveness. Then they may have to go back to learn to *court* each other again; learn to talk to each other again; learn to touch and learn to love in new and exciting ways. God wants partners to take time to communicate and express their love physically, respecting each others needs and wishes at all times.

'The Bible has plenty to say about this. *The husband should fulfil his marital duty to his wife and likewise the wife to her husband..*' (I Cor. 7:3). God speaks of honouring one another; seeing our bodies as 'temples' of the Holy Spirit; but it is not something many couples feel free to talk about until things go drastically wrong.'

It is said that the British try to avoid discussing religion, politics and sex. Christians should, of course, talk about their faith, not simply dry 'religion' and the church seems to be saying more and more about politics these days. If we are honest, however, most of us still hold to that final taboo. In an age when immorality and infidelity are portrayed as the norm, there is increasing pressure to conform to the ways of the world. We know that we should be taking a stand, pointing the way but, just as it was when our children asked that awkward question about sex at an inconvenient moment, we sheepishly admit that we would really prefer it if someone else came up with the answers for us.

The last thing Meg Duncan would ever claim to have is 'all the answers'. But she knows Someone who can point the way. Her ministry is one from which the majority of us might shrink, either out of a feeling of inadequacy or out of sheer embarrassment. She tells of the occasion when one of her married daughters, as a deliberate conversation stopper, when asked what her mother did, replied, 'Oh, she is a sex therapist!'

50

All joking apart, however, we live in an age when sexual infidelity is creating havoc in marriages and untold stress in our children. It is also a time when the whole institution of the family is under threat and the church needs to do more than preach about it from the pulpit.

The timely work that Meg is doing may not merit headline news as something which is causing a moral revolution in the world today but, in her own small corner, she is bravely speaking out and actively helping couples to face up to the uncomfortable facts of life, which so many of us would like simply and quietly to go away by prayer alone.

3
Called to Serve

Whether it be the occasional comment by a politician on the radio, a lurid story in the tabloid press or simply a television comedy, the British Civil Service is often at the receiving end of our cynical comments. Perhaps it is because we believe that the 'conspiracy theory' may be more fact than fiction, a suspicion fuelled by the Official Secrets Act and convention which seal the lips of all civil servants asked to confirm or deny any controversial rumour.

Dr Neil Summerton, a senior civil servant in Whitehall for many years, is very clear about his role, and the commitment to serving the Government of the day which is central to his job. We spent some time together discussing this and he spoke of his writings on the subject.

In 'A Mandarin's Duty', a paper published in the journal *Parliamentary Affairs* in 1980, Neil expressed his opinions succinctly.

'It is the civil servant's duty to give with courage, honesty, integrity and clarity the advice which he believes to be right on the basis of his experience and knowledge and the facts of the case in so far as he can ascertain them. He is not free simply to tell the minister what he thinks the latter wants to hear, especially if that entails any misrepresentation of what he believes or knows to be the facts. Nor is he free to abstain from giving advice because it might be disagreeable to the minister.'

These principles are also reflected in his own personal life and witness outside the world of work. Although his job takes up a considerable amount of his time, doing work which he thoroughly enjoys, his colleagues know that there are many other things to occupy his attention. His Christian life and service in his local church are not just diversions at weekends to take his mind off the pressures of business. Without this important focus, which includes being a congregational leader and preacher, he is in no doubt that his life would not be so fulfilled. He believes also that his faith is a source of strength and guidance when faced with dilemmas he encounters from time to time.

'When I look back on my life, I realise that things could have been very different. I am by nature very ambitious. Study, daily work and many other diversions could have taken up all my time over many years, had I not encountered Christ at a particular juncture in my youth.'

Born in Lincolnshire during World War 2, he lived most of his childhood in the West Midlands in an ordinary lower middle class home. His parents sent him to a local Church of England three-teacher primary school, where he was one of only forty pupils.

'My mother, who died some years ago, was an active churchgoer from her youth in an Anglo-Catholic parish and I am sure that she was a believer. My father did not have the same commitment at that early stage, although it is hard really to know how he stood as far as his faith was concerned, until after I became a Christian. I was sent to Sunday School and taken to church most week-ends. This, together with some of the religious instruction I received at school, provided me with a good introduction to the Bible and many aspects of the Christian faith. I had an enquiring mind and, unlike some of the other boys, did not find R.E. a turn-off.'

He made excellent progress at school and succeeded in passing his 'eleven-plus' at the age of nine, when he transferred to grammar school in Shropshire.

At the age of thirteen he became less interested in church and, like so many teenagers, began to look elsewhere for fulfilment. He did attend the Christian Union in his school run by two of the masters and this provided him with food for thought, particularly as he read the Scripture Union Notes most nights. But the Christian faith had no particular meaning for him at that stage. Being an intelligent young man, he began to question what life was all about. What is the significance of the Universe? What is the significance of human existence? Is there a God?

'I began to reflect on what the world was all about and wrestled with these questions. I kept them to myself, inevitably considering them against the background of the Christian teaching I had received.

'Questioning about the nature of life and eternal things plagued me during my early teenage years until, at the age of fifteen, all I can say is that God met me: not that I had a vision or any great supernatural experience, as some do. I vividly recall in November, 1956 going between classes in school when I was gripped with a palpable sense of judgment. This was not the result of any great sermon or something said to me that morning: it was just a piercing sense of conviction of sin; a realisation that I was not ready to meet God should something happen to me. I can only attribute this to the Holy Spirit working in my life.'

The experience remained in his mind but he took no immediate action on it. Two months after the unusual occurrence in the school corridor, Neil, who was also a keen member of the Boy Scouts, attended an activity weekend with them at a RAF base. One evening they ran a 'brains trust' and somebody slipped in a question for the members of the panel, '*Are you a Christian? and if not, why not?*' The panel and audience discussed it and were floundering around until the chairman pointed out that the main problem was that they could not define what was meant by 'a Christian'.

'To everyone's surprise, he suggested that we should ask the forces' chaplain who happened to be in the audience. He turned out to be David Pawson, a Baptist minister doing his military service at the time. He only said two sentences to explain that a Christian is someone who believed that Jesus Christ died for their sin.'

It was like a light being turned on in Neil's mind. Suddenly, he understood for the first time why Christ died and, above all, that he had died for him: previously, that had seemed like a surplus piece in the jigsaw, an awful mistake, rather than the central explanatory fact.

He was still unsure what he needed to do to respond to this ultimate sacrifice: it was another month before things had fallen into place and he recognised that he had been converted.

'At that point, God made necessary arrangements for growth in this new faith: within a few weeks I was invited to attend a regular weekly "at home" for teenagers in the village, run by a couple who were Christians and had an engineering business in the area.'

Because of that contact, Jack and Isobel Stordy were to become his spiritual parents. At a Bible Study in their home, the gospel message became clear to him and the foundations of his Christian life were laid.

'These were days when I was nurtured in the faith as a young believer and I grew from day to day as I read the Bible and had fellowship in their home. They also used to run after-church rallies in the village hall, opposed then by the local Anglican priest who viewed evangelical lay people with suspicion: those were days when the established church still had a certain power and influence in rural society.

'We also attended house parties at Hildenborough Hall to hear Tom Rees, who had a great teaching ministry. Young Christians in particular were greatly helped by his preaching and Bible studies and I was no exception. Nine months after I became a Christian, I realised at one of these weeks that, while I was quite content for God to take my sin to guarantee me eternal life, I was not so sure about giving my mind and my intellect to him, perhaps to take advantage of it in ways that might be inconvenient.

That summer the words of the hymn,

> Take my life and let it be
> Consecrated Lord to thee . . .
> Take my intellect and use
> Every power as thou shalt choose.

became my prayer.'

As if to test his commitment, immediately afterwards, for a whole year, Neil was plagued with enormous intellectual doubts, and even questioned the existence of a God in a world of war and turmoil.

'This was a wilderness experience of great anguish for me and I know that had I not met Christ before it all, and come to learn more about the Word of God, I might easily have slipped into atheism. But I had had an experience which I knew was real and I came out of these dark days much stronger in my faith than before. Of enormous support to me during this period were the writings of C.S. Lewis, in particular *The Screwtape Letters* and *Mere Christianity*.

'As well, taking Tom Rees' advice, I had started learning the scriptures by heart and set myself the challenge of memorising the book of Romans.'

This proved to be a source of strength which helped him to establish his faith in Christ. He also appreciated during this time the significance of parts of the Anglican Order of Service which he had known from his childhood.

'In particular, the phrase from Cranmer's Second Collect at Morning Prayer, "Whose service is perfect freedom", came home to me and I realised that my life would never be completely fulfilled and "free" unless I was fully committed to serve and follow him.'

His academic work progressed at a pace, studying History, Latin and French at A-level. Perhaps under the influence of the headmaster, a historian, he was persuaded that History was his forte and considered it as a possible subject for a university degree. His ambition on leaving school was to get into Oxford but he failed to do so, much to the surprise of his parents and his masters. A place was offered at King's College, London to read History.

Although Neil still values many of the foundations provided for him by the Anglican church, as he studied the Tudor and Stuart period of church history, he began to doubt the principle of establishment. He came to believe that the whole structure, with the state supporting the church, seemed very much to be a 'political fix', to use his words.

Through Jack and Isobel Stordy he had also come into contact with more radical views of the local church as a gathering of believers, as practised among the Christian Brethren, a comparatively small but influential group among evangelicals.

When he went to London University he attended the Christian Union and became an office-holder but found little Christian nourishment there. Along with a number of other students, he went along to a local congregation of the Christian Brethren tradition, Cholmeley Evangelical Church, in Highgate, north London.

'Leaving home I found London to be a rather inhospitable place and I felt more like a commuter than a student when I was living there. There was no real university life, so the church, which was full of young people at that time, turned out to be a haven. Their form of worship and government was a sharp contrast with my Anglican upbringing but I felt that it matched my already-formed opinions on the established church. What was then a reflection of my intellectual opinions, developed into a wider understanding of the basic principles of the New Testament Church: the gathering of God's people, a fluid and flexible organism, rather than an institution or an organisation.

'However, this is not to say that I thought, or think, that the Church is other than all Christian believers, whatever their denominational tag. I hold no brief for the Christian Brethren as a perfect form of Christianity!'

This was to be the beginning of over 32 years of service in many spheres of the life of the fellowship which extended such a warm welcome to him in his student days. He met his wife there and over the years was instrumental, with her and with others, in organising outreach among young people in particular. There they were associated through family and friends with the beginnings of Musical Gospel Outreach and Buzz Magazine, which were among the source organisations leading to activities today such as Spring Harvest.

When they got married in 1965 they wanted very much to live in the area but property was more than they could afford. They made it a matter for prayer as they felt that God wanted them to work in this church.

'We were driving along the road when my wife noticed a house for sale within the area we had drawn on the map. It was an excellent house in a good location. But I knew that it would be way beyond our income and I felt that there was no point even in enquiring. She is a sales person, however, a deal-maker, and she rose to the challenge. She contacted the sellers and, of course, came back with a figure far beyond our means. "I told you so," I said, but she insisted in making a bid within our limits. To my surprise, and an answer to prayer as far as she was concerned, we got it for 60% of the asking price! Our two sons, Ian and Matthew, were brought up there and it is still our home today.'

Earlier, at university he had other decisions to make, for he was unsure what line of study he should follow in History. After a discussion with the reader in Military History, Michael Howard, subsequently Regius Professor of Modern History at Oxford, he opted to study the subject.

Under this excellent teacher he found the study of war to be much more interesting than some had suggested it might be. He came to realise how regrettably fundamental war and violence are to human society; one of the great catalysts with an enormous influence for social, political and economic change.

'As a Christian I had to come to terms with this, in a society which saw its political freedom as based on constant readiness to make war of the most drastic kind - paradoxically, with the whole object of avoiding such a war. This led me to grapple with the then neglected subject of the ethics of war, on which I have written a number of essays over the years.'

In his essay, *The just war: a sympathetic critique*, (from *Pacifism and War*, Leicester: The Inter-Varsity Press, 1984) Neil considers the two main questions specifically addressed in the volume as a whole: "In the biblical understanding, is war a legitimate instrument of state? And if it is, may the Christian consent to and participate in its use?"

These are questions which many of us like to pose but, more often than not, we may prefer to ignore unpalatable answers. Anyone reading this essay cannot but be challenged by the complexity of the issues. I certainly was. But his interest in this field of study extends beyond his writings.

'I was also honorary secretary for seven years of the Council for Christian Approaches to Defence and Disarmament which is a group of officials, military personnel, academics, theologians and churchmen which has provided a forum for discussion on the ethics of war over the last thirty years.

'At the same time, I have been an official in the Department of the Environment so I have had the great privilege of grappling intellectually with the two great issues of our time; war and the environment.

'I feel that it is so important for Christians to have a voice in the area of ethics in our society. As an intellectual and a historian I am not only intensely interested but also feel that I should try to contribute to the debate, given the knowledge and experience which has been entrusted to me. So as I move round the Department - land use one year, the aquatic environment another - I try, if I can, to find a way of teasing out on paper some of the theological, philosophical and ethical principles which are relevant.'

He enjoyed being an undergraduate but, after qualifying in 1963, he was still unsure what he wanted to do with his life and asked God to give him some direction.

'I remember talking to Professor Michael Howard,

who was interested to know whether I wanted to go on to do research. When I told him that all depended on what God wanted me to do with my life, and he did not seem to think me totally strange for putting it that way, I decided to prepare a PhD thesis on the Development of British Military Planning for a War against Germany, 1904-1914 - chosen partly in order to research something as near to the present day as possible.'

He hesitated for a time about whether he should seek a post in university teaching and research as an academic, but his wish to do something more practical with his life won. In 1965 he decided to take the civil service examinations and was accepted to enter as soon as he had completed the research for his PhD, so he took success in the exams as God's way of guiding him.

In 1966 he joined the Ministry of Transport and embarked on a career which he was to find challenging, interesting and rewarding. In the early years, he worked on matters such as Highways Policy, Passenger Transport, Freight Transport etc. and during that period took further studies to progress in the service.

In the mid 1970s, he was responsible for policy on industrial and commercial property development - at the time when the Labour Party was making its third attempt to deal with the vexed question of development values. In the early 1980s he implemented the Conservative Government's right to buy council houses and, more recently, the highly controversial Community Charge, or Poll Tax, as it became known.

At the moment he is the Head of the Water Directorate in the Department of the Environment. All these jobs have entailed giving policy advice to ministers and implementing their policy decisions.

'Ministers when elected to office nearly always see themselves as committed to change. They see their role as making the machine of government work better under them than it did under their predecessor even if he or she was of the same party. If you were to ask me why I joined the civil service and why I feel privileged to hold this position, it is because I feel that I have the important task of helping to make things "work better".

'The commitment of the service to give unstinting intellectual support to the Government of the day is central to the smooth functioning of government as we know it in this country. Of course, that is not to say that advice is always welcome: as in any walk of life, those in charge sometimes wish that their advisers had better news.

'The work is so varied that it is very difficult to be bored as one simply does not know what will turn up next. I have found myself over the years being incredibly busy, perhaps pre-occupied with my career. There is the constant danger that other priorities in my life are not attended to. As I look back I now realise that I spent a lot of time studying, working in my office and then returning home to my family only to go out again on some work connected with the church.

'It is possible to be a Christian workaholic and, frankly, I do not feel that I was a very good father to my boys; although I always saw them to bed at night I did not take much time to play with them. Reading and praying with them most nights were important and I am glad I took time to do that. But, if I had it all to live over again, I hope I would spend more time with my children.

I regard myself as fortunate that our boys have followed us in Christian commitment - it's better than I deserved.

'When it comes to priorities, the work that I do for the Kingdom of God and his people is more important than what I do in the office. Like Paul, I see my job as "tent making", a means of earning money to live. But that does not mean that I serve the country in a half-hearted way. It is the opposite, in fact, as I believe I am called to serve God and honour him in all facets of my life. I am sure that Paul's tents were the best on the market. I try to make my "products" that too!'

At one point early on, still unsure whether he was to be an administrator or an academic, and daunted by the thought of working in the civil service for the remainder of his career, he left to spend four years at King's College, working direct to the Principal, General Sir John Hackett. His role was as policy and corporate planner for the college. It was inspiring to work with Sir John but he missed policy-making at the Government level and it was not easy to make a coherent career in university administration at that time.

'Although it appears to have been an unnecessary interruption to my professional progress, I now believe that it was a correct move to make, given my home and family circumstances at the time. The children were very small and Pauline was under a lot of pressure, as she had had to take over the family business when her father took ill and then died. Coincidentally, she had a bad ectopic pregnancy and almost died herself. If I had been in the civil service during that period, I am certain I would not have been with her at the critical moment when the fallopian tube burst, requiring me to rush her to hospital in my own car.

'I have often wondered whether I did the right thing to try to switch careers. The lesson for me, however, is that whether or not I did stray from God's will, he brought some good out of it, despite me.

'I have heard many sermons on the subject of God's will and have preached on it myself; knowing his will and walking in it is not as easy to do as some Christians simplistically maintain. I believe Christians and churches often force God to take the long way round. I often struggle with whether my motive is selfish ambition or the desire to put to good use the talents and spiritual gifts that God has given me.'

His return to the civil service was very much influenced by a desire to get involved again in the political administrative process. This was the element he missed most during his short venture at the university.

'It is hard for the layman to understand but, being a civil servant is very much like being both an observer with a grandstand seat and a participant in a sport. Not only do you feel involved on the field but also as a privileged spectator of events at the national level.'

Neil wittily described being a policy-making civil servant as 'a cross between being a monk and Mr Hudson' (the head butler in the famous TV drama *Upstairs Downstairs*). A monk because of the disciplined commitment, the sense of vocation shared with committed colleagues in an essentially collegiate rather than competitive atmosphere; Mr Hudson because, although definitely "downstairs" in terms of real power and authority, the family often depended on his professional commitment, competence and counsel.

'The ethic which I outlined in *A Mandarin's Duty* in 1979 was not my invention but an attempt to distil the tradition as it had developed over more than a century - to set down the beginning of a code which has often been called for since. To my mind at least, the unusual role given to the British civil service is easier to accept if one is Christian because there is a parallel with serving God. Moreover, government is given a special position under God in scripture. I am called to serve in both kingdoms. In neither context is one left simply to follow one's own bright ideas!'

The role he is called on to fulfil can lead to real stress and pressure. These arise not just from the chemistry of relationships with ministers and colleagues - that he notes is common to all workplace situations. In this case, however, there can be the stress of working on issues of fundamental political debate, like the right to buy, poll tax, or Europe. It is not always easy when, as he humorously put it, he is, like a midwife, called to deliver what someone else has conceived when, to many, it has been misconceived!

'The British civil servant is highly privileged since he remains in post whatever the colour of the government. In most other countries these are politically selected positions and the personnel change with the election of each new government. Being permanent, our job is to give faithful and committed service to the government of the day. It is not simply to be neutral for, provided the government is constitutionally elected, it is our job to do what they want to do and it would actually be unethical for us to oppose them, even if personally or practically we might disagree with them.

Competence without political conviction is what we are required to provide, though inevitably things are usually better done if one believes they are worth doing.

'But such an arrangement could be lethal if some day government were to fall into the wrong hands. The question sometimes occurs to me: in what circumstances would civil servants be justified in drawing the line? (Such circumstances must be possible because the rules do actually make provision for them.) I sometimes pray that I will recognise when it would be right to take a stand if as a civil servant I were tempted to go beyond my duty - it would certainly be necessary to keep one's wits about one, because such is life and the political process that one cannot guarantee that they would immediately be recognisable.

'I thank God for the country we live in but one need only think back to those who served in Germany early in the 1930s - a civilised democracy at the time. To what extent did public servants fail to recognise what was happening until it was too late to do anything about it? Constitutionally we are richly blessed. But we dare not regard ourselves as immune from such risks simply because this is the United Kingdom - but, after all, wasn't it said long ago that the price of freedom is eternal vigilance. If such circumstances were ever to arise, I pray that God will give civil servants the wisdom to know, and the boldness to make a stand, when policy and decisions are so morally wrong that they are not entitled to claim the obedience of civil servants.'

This, however, is the extreme and happily hypothetical case. The familiar area of moral challenge day in and day out for Neil is, rather, the issue of truth, particularly in defending and advocating policy positions. The reality of the debate about policy in a democratic society, he says, is that different groups often take up opposing positions and advocate them publicly. Increasingly this debate is conducted from day to day in the press and electronic media, in what Neil has sometimes called, echoing his background in war studies, 'the information firefight'.

From one point of view this creates a healthy tension in a democratic society. But all involved in it are exposed to temptations to put the argument so as to present one's own position in the best light. The cut and thrust of public debate lends itself to exaggeration of one's own position, and to selection of material to support it. In the process, truth could easily be an early casualty.

This is in fact a real problem for journalists and lobby groups just as much as for civil servants. The Government, however, is rightly required to be committed to the highest standards in this area. The assumption of the constitution is that truth is indispensable and in principle knowable, even if imperfectly, rather than a relative commodity which can be sacrificed if the end seems noble enough.

If this were not demanding enough, Neil believes that, because of his Christian profession, there is in practice bound to be a special requirement on him of integrity of argument within the Department and in explaining policies publicly.

'The goal must be to argue, in as clear and truthful a way as possible, within the inevitable constraints of space. The problem does not of course lie in blatant untruth: it is the grey area of selection of material, which must of course be done anyway in the interests of brevity, simplicity and intelligibility. The risk is of slowly allowing one's standards in this area to slip.

'Against this background, I occasionally have wondered whether there may be times in some societies whether the whole process could become so lacking in truthfulness that anyone with a commitment to absolute values might have to withdraw from it completely. Looking across history, it is clear that there are circumstances in which political cultures can become so deceptive that anyone with a commitment to truth would have to oppose it.'

Neil talked also about the importance of living the Christian life in the office situation. His beliefs are no secret to those above and below him. For this reason his everyday life must reflect his witness, as it is on the practical things that people base their judgment. Truth and fairness are just as important when dealing with staff as they are at meetings with a minister or a lobby group. Encouragement and approval should be given as regularly as one would wish to receive it, if good relationships and exemplary leadership are to be maintained.

'If Christian managers are not fair and honest with their staff, then the whole basis of their Christianity would be dismissed and any witness they tried to maintain would be in vain. I feel that I have many opportunities to witness, and often openings occur if only because it becomes known that I am a member of the Brethren, which to many is identified with a sect which has had a very bad name in the tabloid press over the last 30 years.'

An active member of Cholmeley Evangelical Church

for over 32 years, he is involved in several local and national committees associated with the movement. He is also a member of the Council of the Evangelical Alliance, is chairman of the trustees of the Christian magazine *Aware* and director of London Christian Housing plc., a company which aims to provide housing for full-time Christian workers in London. Regular invitations come in for him to address conferences in the U.K. and abroad.

'There are so many misunderstandings about the denomination that it can also be a conversation stopper! Nevertheless I have never been afraid to speak up about it, if only because it often leads on to serious conversation about the fundamental truths of Christianity, the importance of which far exceeds a denominational tag.

'My aim with my denomination is simply to ensure that local groups of believers make the adaptations needed to maintain that effective witness to Christ. If that means that churches are unrecognisable as 'Brethren', as a result, so be it. My work within the denomination does not aim to preserve it - far from it. It has maintained an excellent witness to Christ for over a hundred years, but God is not committed to denominations and expects them to adapt, not in essential doctrine but in forms and practice to maintain an effective role for Christ according to the needs of the day.

'I believe that the movement, much maligned over the decades for its strong evangelical tradition and outreach, still has a part to play today in the wider scheme of things. This, despite the fact that evangelicals are much more accepted in all of the denominations nowadays. I continue to work in my local church, praying that my vision of revival among its people will come to pass in the near future.'

He is secretary of the Christian Brethren Partnership, which includes members from churches throughout the United Kingdom. It is now expanding to include people from other countries and the need to travel abroad as a civil servant has incidentally given him the opportunity to meet a few key people in Europe. This is one way in which he feels the movement can share ideas and pray together to achieve the goal of renewal.

Among his writings he has debated the effect of the lack of full-time workers within the denomination and he argues that it is an issue which they need to address as they consider their work and witness into the next century (*Servants of God: Papers on the use of full-time workers in Brethren churches*. Christian Brethren Research Journal no 37, Exeter: Paternoster Press 1986).

'We are not a denomination with a tradition of full-time leaders but I feel that we must find ways of generating such ministries as, in our modern society, I believe that it is extremely difficult to cope without them. As each congregation is autonomous, we have no national mechanism to achieve this.'

His educational background, knowledge of good leadership and the skills of diplomacy and communication, central to his day-to-day work, have been effectively applied in his church. Qualities like these have been invaluable to him as an elder and a preacher and he has been able to help others to recognise that relationships with people are crucial to good leadership in the church as are theological knowledge and the ability to construct a sermon. He has written a number of articles on the subject and has summed up his thoughts in a book on eldership and ministry in the local church, *A Noble Task* (Paternoster Press, 1987).

'Our congregation went through a crisis of identity and effectiveness which led many to go elsewhere and perhaps my training and experience helped me to play an important part in the discussions at that time: and still do, for there are continually areas for debate as each new generation considers afresh what the previous one has taken for granted. Numbers fluctuated greatly at that stage and the temptation for many was whether to remain with the congregation or seek pastures new. I felt that God wanted me to stay put and I believe that he enabled me to take a place of leadership which may have saved our congregation from breaking up.

'More recently, God challenged me with the thought that the Church has to shift from "maintenance" to "mission"; to encourage growth and the planting of new churches; and so far as Brethren churches are concerned, to look at the possible role of full-time workers and the training of lay leaders.'

He recalled the support which God gave him at the time of crisis in his life and in the congregation. Late one evening, about fifteen years ago, after a busy day at the office, he was reading the last few verses of John's Gospel to his son Matthew in his bedroom as he went to sleep.

'There are points in my life when I have been aware that God has been dealing direct with me and this was one of them. I felt as if God was in the room and that he was speaking to me, even though my eight-year old son was quite unaware of it. God made it absolutely clear to me that I had to continue to work for him where

I was and I had to commit myself to him again.

'It was at a time when the congregation was in much difficulty and numbers and fellow-leaders were haemorrhaging away, including one of my closest friends. God challenged me as I read the verses aloud to Matthew that their call to go elsewhere for fellowship was not my business, and that the nature of leadership responsibility for me in my mature years was to accept the tasks that my fellowship was giving me: "...*when you were young, you...walked where you would; but when you are old...others will gird you and carry you where you do not wish to go.*"

'Sitting on my son's bed, I knew that, whatever freedom others had, my task was to stay in that congregation. On another occasion, I sensed God telling me personally that "the years that the locusts had eaten" in that service would indisputably be restored to me. My sense of guidance then has been vindicated as the church has moved forward to a period of outreach and extension. Interestingly, as it has done so, my leadership has become much less important as others have come in to support and continue the work of the congregation.'

He firmly believes that the local church has a pivotal part to play in the community today; to give expression to the Kingdom of God not only in the proclamation of the gospel and in worship but also doing good works and living out the gospel in everyday life to demonstrate the essential character of the future kingdom that God has in his plan. By their very presence in society, Christians can help to protect it from the worst evils which may befall it. He is concerned that many evangelicals, dedicated to win souls by the preaching of the gospel, or at the other extreme to get deeply involved in political action, may be ignoring the simple call of Christ to live in and do good works in their community; to be the 'salt of the earth.'

As he pointed out in one of his essays on the just war, if there had been only ten righteous in Sodom, it would have been spared from becoming a paradigm of divine judgment!

Neil Summerton is in all respects a typical civil servant. He is meticulous in his attention to detail, ever conscious of the privilege of his position and dedicated to serve his country to the best of his ability. It is a job he loves to do but, as he has clearly explained, his service goes above and beyond the call of duty.

After an interesting morning of discussion and fellowship with him I was left in no doubt that it is the spiritual dimension to his dedication which makes everything worthwhile; and his life all the more fulfilled as a result.

4

A Bedside Manner

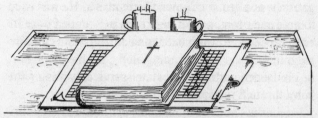

'Mr Fraser, can you come immediately to the Special Care Baby Unit? We've a baby recently born with a serious condition and his mother is requesting baptism.'

'Of course, I'm on my way,' he replied and hung up without wasting time by asking the reason for the urgency.

He moved speedily out of the ward and across the hospital to the Unit. The Special Care Baby Unit was well lit and warm. In a side ward, gowned figures clustered round one of the incubators. A young mother in her dressing gown sat closely, anxiously looking on. A staff midwife spoke to her quietly. Seeing Arthur approach, she stood up and introduced him to the mother. He then crossed over to the doctor who explained the situation, briefly and simply. 'He's not got much of a chance.'

Nothing in his theological training had prepared him for this. Neither was there an Order of Service available for such an eventuality. There was no time to question the nature of the Sacrament, or its significance, in these circumstances. He had committed many an infant into the hands of the Lord and his Church. But the contrast was stark. The solemnity and serenity of a church building were replaced by the bright lights, the hustle and bustle of a hospital ward. There were no rows of doting relatives only a mother barely awake; the congregation was a group of gowned attendants. He was used to an ornate font, with a napkin neatly draped over its edge. Instead, he was handed a small foil basin containing a little water and, standing alongside the incubator, he proceeded with an abbreviated service, baptising the baby through the small porthole.

'...in the name of the Father, the Son and the Holy Spirit.' Even as he spoke the familiar words and touched the tiny forehead, he was unsure what they really meant in this context, for there were no vows, no promises and no congregation present to welcome the young one into their fellowship.

The blessing given, he closed the porthole, moved to the weeping mother's side and the staff resumed their care. No music, no baptismal certificate, no congratulations; it had taken three minutes. Later he would talk to the young mother more fully; all the time asking God for words to say, words to comfort, when aspirations, lovingly gathered during nine months of patient waiting, had been so coldly and suddenly shattered.

For Arthur Fraser the realities of suffering, death and the joys of recovery and new found life, are a regular occurrence. As chaplain to the hospitals in Inverness, his workload is as varied and demanding as any profession but it is the spiritual dimension to his occupation which sets him apart in so many ways from other personnel. This dimension has its rewards, of course, as people are sustained and blessed by the gifts which God has given him. But it also brings him face to face with challenges to his faith, not only in the circumstances of death and bereavement he encounters, but also in the sorrow, disillusionment and occasional bitterness which he meets in people from time to time.

Few people really know what the job of hospital chaplain entails. In fact, Arthur himself confesses to finding the job much more varied than he had at first anticipated. Most people imagine a chaplain to be a minister who goes round the wards, speaking words of comfort and perhaps taking a service on a Sunday morning. As I spoke with him, I too was amazed at the breadth of activities he engaged in.

We met first on a Saturday morning in one of the little rooms next to the hospital chapel. He was on duty and had his pager in his breast pocket, ready to respond if necessary to any call. During our time together I was to learn more about his job and the blessings which he has had from the ministry. Ever conscious of breaching confidentiality, he recounted to me many more stories; some sad, some very funny and recalled for me how his life and work in God's service had prepared him for the work he does today. An interesting testimony unfolded.

He was brought up in a caring home where his parents sent him to Sunday School although they themselves were irregular attenders at the local church. The death of his father during the war was a great blow to the family and any faith that his mother had, diminished in the sense of loss and abandonment which she felt in her grief. This faith was to be rekindled in later life but not soon enough to be of any strength to her young son.

A bit of a renegade, he soon stopped going to Sunday

School. However, more to escape from the boredom of a Scottish Sunday and meet his school friends than to learn about the Bible, he was attracted to a local Bible class organised by the Crusaders. For whatever reason he ventured out every Sunday afternoon, God had other plans for him. Little by little, impressed by the sincerity of the lay leaders of the class, many of whom he had come to know and admire at school, he was indeed learning about the Bible. It was some years later, at a Scripture Union Camp in St Andrews, a university town on the east coast of Scotland, that he remembers all that he had learned at Crusaders coming together in a challenge to commit his life to Christ.

'The lesson was about Barabbas and the choice given to the crowd before the crucifixion of Jesus,' he recalled. 'While I did not shout for Barabbas, I was aware that I was not one of those who had chosen Christ. Silence was not a confession of support. That was a turning point in my life and the moment I believe I committed myself to Christ.'

He had no sooner left school in 1951, when he was called up to join the RAF. His plea for a compassionate posting to Scotland to be with his widowed mother was ignored and, after initial training, he ultimately found himself with a flight which operated from Amman in Jordan. Service life proved a challenge to the faith of many young Christians in those days and it was no less so for Arthur. His early attendance at local churches when in training, however, marked him out and each evening he became aware that other young men were trying to witness as they read their Bibles and prayed at their bedside. Impressed by their fortitude, despite jeers and boots being sent in their direction, Arthur soon realised that he had to show whose side he was on.

In Jordan, he was associated with other Christians who worked consistently with the service personnel. Not least among them, he remembers General Glubb of the Arab Legion who introduced him to many fine believers. One in particular, Jack Blockley, a local schoolteacher, arranged services in the camp. He befriended the young conscript, taught him the importance of the devotional life for a Christian and encouraged him to witness to his faith.

He met many Christians among the officers and men and also became involved in local services for the servicemen and the Arab population. They put on a series of Fact and Faith films in the camp cinema and he looks back fondly on many an evening of sharing his faith in the local churches.

'Oh yes, they joked and teased me from time to time. Most of it was good humoured and, as a result, I found that they would come to me with their personal problems - discreetly asking me to "put up a wee prayer".'

The offer to 'put up a wee prayer' was to become the catchphrase with which the men who sought his counsel would associate him and again to be repeated at many a bedside in later years. Although he did not realise it at the time, Arthur was being gently introduced to a pastoral ministry which would serve as a foundation for much of the work he would do in the future.

The troubles in the Middle East in those days led to the occasional reprisal and, from time to time, he was confronted with the death of a colleague. Sometimes he would be asked to read the lesson at a funeral, or some other service, alongside the chaplains, whose work he admired and respected.

Unlike many other conscripts, Arthur did not particularly look forward to being demobbed. In the RAF he had travelled, met adventure and, above all, had made many fine friends who had helped him to grow in the faith. Although he considered joining up as a regular, he found himself back in Glasgow training to be a fire surveyor and assessor with an insurance company. It may have seemed appropriate for him to consider going in for the ministry at that point in his life but this was not so, as he explained.

'My idea was that I would earn a good living, settle down and join a local church where I could worship and work for the Lord. The work and witness of Scripture Union and Crusaders, which had so influenced me as a young man, stuck in my mind. I wanted to join with them in their outreach - but part-time, as a layman. Full time Christian work was far from my thoughts then.'

Things changed, however, in 1955, the year of the Billy Graham Crusade, which took Scotland - indeed Britain - by storm. Arthur did not miss a single night during the six weeks of the campaign! He was engaged as a counsellor and was privileged to speak to many people, leading them to a further knowledge of Christ.

The Crusade fired many young people to consider full-time work. In fact, it could be said that many jumped in with both feet, without considering the full implications of their commitment. Lorne Sanney, one of the Crusade workers, later director of the Navigators, held special meetings for young men. Arthur remembers one meeting in particular.

'Lorne spoke that evening from Isaiah and the verse, *Here am I Lord, send me.* But he said that, with so many young women now working in Christian service, the verse to that gathering was more like, *Here am I Lord, send my sister*! The message was not lost in the humour and I was challenged by it.'

He spoke to his minister, Ernest Watson of Knightswood United Free Church. To his surprise, he was none too encouraging. Not to be put off so easily, he sought 'a second opinion' in Scripture Union's J. W. ('Boss') Meiklejohn. He did not encourage him either!

Thinking back on the event, Arthur now knows what was happening. 'They were testing me. So many young people did not think carefully about what they were doing. They wanted to change the world - like Billy Graham. I was one of many who had spoken to those men of God and I was reminded, "If you don't get the call right, nothing else will be right".'

In time, after much thought and prayer, Arthur applied to become a minister with the United Free Church. His studies took him to Edinburgh to the University, the U.F. College and New College.

In 1960, the same year that he married his wife, Marion, he was called to North Woodside United Free Church, Glasgow. In those formative years of his ministry he was supported by experienced elders and learned so much about the importance of being open to listen to all shades of opinion in the Church. He learned that God was bigger than denominations and, more importantly, larger than his own Christian life to date.

In 1966, in a move which happened almost before he realised it, he found himself in charge of a church extension in the new Drumchapel housing estate, one of many set up in the city to meet the chronic shortage of homes after the war. This proved to be one of the most challenging times in his ministry. The work was a sharp contrast to North Woodside, which was a long established parish. In Drumchapel, along with other denominations in different 'zones' of the town, his congregation was a social mix and included many people rehoused from the city centre.

Members came from city missions, including the famous Tent and Bethany Halls. The outreach was interdenominational and, at times, non-denominational. New Christians brought to the faith through workers' Christian fellowships in the shipyards and at the Singer sewing machine factory, came along with their refreshing attitude to the faith. They had to be ministered to alongside others well-versed in the Bible. To put it another way, some were learning to dive and life-save while others were barely swimming.

Supported by young people from the Inter-Varsity Fellowship and by teams from the Bible Training Institute and the Worldwide Evangelisation Crusade, the work expanded rapidly and led him to reconsider many things he had taken for granted.

'Although a committed member of the United Free Church, I was never a narrow denominationalist. I suppose my SU and Crusader work, as well as my time in the RAF when basic beliefs were more important than denominational tags, account for this. But during my time at Drumchapel, meeting people of all ages from so many church backgrounds, and from abroad, I began to question many things.

'I became aware that the gospel was wider than some of my Christian friends believed. Yes, there is a need for a personal encounter with Christ. There is a command to win people by the preaching of the Word, but our church outreach found us painting kitchens, digging gardens and helping to clothe our neighbours. The "social gospel", wrongly maligned by some evangelicals, was an essential part of our work - and we had to show that it wasn't just to bribe them to come to church. This experience was later to have a deeper significance in my work as hospital chaplain today.'

Hospital visiting was a key part of the work Arthur did and one which he particularly enjoyed. He recalls learning so much about the fortitude of patients and the special kind of ministry to those who felt weak and vulnerable, whatever their age, church affiliation or professional status. When the chaplaincy at a city hospital came up, it seemed right to apply; but he was not successful.

'In retrospect, I suppose, God was not saying "No!", but "Not yet, Arthur!" for I had much more to learn and do before I came to this charge. I found myself working in a children's home but not before many questions - and tempting alternatives - were put to me.'

In his youth, Arthur allowed his widowed mother to have the odd evening out by baby-sitting his wee brother. On these occasions he would read or listen to the radio. Even before he became interested in spiritual things, he enjoyed hearing about the dramatic adventures of people like David Livingstone, Eric Liddell and William Quarrier. When the post in the well-known Quarrier's Homes in central Scotland was advertised he applied and, after many discussions and enquiries by the directors, he was invited to join them.

The invitation reached him in Canada where, as President of Scottish Christian Endeavour, he was attending their World Convention. The reply was not an easy one for, on top of it all, he had been invited to take over a church there. After much prayer, he accepted the call to Quarrier's in 1970.

The seven years spent there were memorable. Witnessing the dedication of the staff and working with so many young people in need of love and care, widened his horizons even further and confirmed, if it needed to be, his conviction that the love of Christ was indeed wider than many try to make it. The simple chorus he had sung so many times in Scripture Union camps around Scotland, took on a deeper meaning now.

> Wide wide as the ocean,
> High as the heavens above,
> Deep, deep as the deepest sea,
> Is my Saviour's love.
> I, though so unworthy,
> Still am a child of his care,
> For his Word teaches me,
> That his love reaches me,
> Everywhere.

There came a time when his period of service at Quarrier's was coming to an end - he had already accepted two, three-year contracts - and he began to consider other Christian service. It was during this period when the chaplaincy at Inverness in the Highlands became vacant and he applied for the post.

'By coincidence - if God believes in such a thing -

my wife and I were on holiday in St. Andrews, where that turning point in my life took place so many years before, when I was called to Inverness for an interview,' Arthur related. 'I remember coming out of the Royal Northern Infirmary and saying to Marion, who is a General Practitioner and no stranger to hospitals, "Well, dear, how would you like to live in Inverness?" and that was the start of what has been one of the most fulfilling times in my ministry.

'I suppose I once thought also that the job of hospital chaplain was about visiting people at their bedside - and it is indeed central to the work - but there is more, much more, than most people realise.'

An important part of his work is the training of part-time chaplains to assist in the hospitals as the work is more than one man alone can cope with. He is ably assisted by his colleague, Derek Brown, a tower of strength to him in times of stress and a friend to pray with and share the day's happenings.

Arthur lectures to nurses in training; not sermons, he stresses, but a series of talks to make them consider the spiritual dimension of the human being. He illustrates this by showing the interrelated circles of BODY, MIND AND SPIRIT.

It can be quite a challenge for a nurse in training, thinking mainly of the physical care of patients, to be called to a bedside, perhaps in the middle of the night, and be told, 'I feel I am dying and need God. I haven't been to church since I was a child. Will you read the Bible to me and pray with me?' She might call for the chaplain, of course, but, after all, she has been caring in other ways for the patient. She has got to know the person well and is trusted by him. Neither can she dismiss his request for it is her duty to support those in her care within all three dimensions. This may not be easy and it is these issues that Arthur discusses with the trainees.

'Not all of them are convinced at the beginning about my input. In fact, some admit to thinking it was a "bit of a yawn" at the time. Generally, though, even the most openly atheistic, are different people after their first spell or two on wards when the realities of life and death confront them.'

On the other hand, there are the nurses who are committed Christians, who readily accept the spiritual dimension which Arthur speaks of in lectures. For their part, they have to learn that many aspects of the faith are not straightforward and that it is not their job primarily to ensure that every non-committed patient should experience a deathbed conversion. However, their life and witness may well have an impact on those in their care.

'I have spoken to one or two young nurses more than a little hurt, if not disillusioned, by the dramatic change which may come over once gentle and lovely people affected by the deterioration of mind and body through disease or treatment. It is certainly disturbing when a gentle old lady, whom you have come to love and respect, turns without warning into a troublesome, screaming patient,' Arthur explained. 'But part of my job is to help student nurses to come to terms with this sort of thing.'

The relationship which he has with the staff is a vital one for they also must trust him and be able to confide in him when necessary. They are human beings too who are not immune from the pain of suffering and death. It can affect their lives and relationships and they often come to talk things over with him.

'No matter how often a doctor has seen a child being born, he is still overjoyed at the birth of his own son or daughter and wishes to share that joy with someone. Many times doctors and nurses finally pull the sheet over the head of a deceased patient and must get on with the job of caring for the living. But the pain of losing a close relative is no less acute for them because of their job and they, in turn, may need counselling.'

Many doctors and nurses question the veracity of the Christian faith and naturally stress the physical and psychological dimensions instead, but few have ever, openly at least, denied the importance of the work that the chaplain does. Most, in fact, see him not as an optional extra but an essential complement to their work.

On more than one occasion, when Arthur has re- marked at the excellent recovery of a patient and has commented on the skills of a trained surgeon, he has been encouraged to be told, 'I may have held the scalpel but God does the healing.'

The realisation that Arthur is not just some pious Holy Joe on call when all else fails, is good for relation- ships. He has to do his bit in hospital social events, like fetes and concerts.

'Not long after I arrived I was quite surprised to be asked to do the Toast to the Lassies at a staff Burns Supper. Now, I'm not a great fan of the bard, nor am I very good at it, but I proposed the toast, nevertheless. It was a sign of my being one of the hospital community.'

The staff also appreciate his lively wit and sense of humour. 'Good for life,' says Arthur, 'but essential for hospital life!' This is exemplified in a trick they played on him.

He was doing the rounds in the Intensive Treatment Unit, when he was advised to go to Cubicle 7, the one furthest from the Nursing Station. A Mrs McPhee would benefit from a visit. The name didn't ring a bell as someone he had met recently, but he went along to the room. The lights had been dimmed, her back was to him and she lay very still. Thinking that she may be asleep, he quietly approached the reclining form in the bed and whispered, 'Hello, Mrs McPhee, are you awake?'

He had no sooner neared the bedside when, to his great surprise, the room filled with a blaze of light and an audience of nurses shouted, 'April fool!' The sleeping mound was none other than a dummy, dressed for the occasion!

Such memorable humorous incidents can be a relief. More often than not, however, they are provided, often unwittingly, by the patients themselves. Take the time when an old lady said to him, 'You know, Mr Fraser, I'm fair dying to get out of this place.' Another lady gaily remarked that she had received, 'A lovely bunch of anenemas from her visitor.'

A young married man in for a 'minor' operation, casually said to the other males in the ward, 'I should be home tonight. After all, I am only here for a vivisection!'

Patients get medical terms confused and say them wrongly. He has been assured that there really is no disease called 'Arthuritis' even after he has visited the bedside!

While a good sense of humour has on more than one occasion helped, if not saved, his day it also serves to relieve the frequent stressful situations he encounters. Most traumatic is the death of a child; hard for any adult to accept it always causes shock and acute distress to the parents.

Arthur knows only too well that words of comfort can sound trite and sincerity is of the essence. He recalls some particularly dramatic and distressing events involving the death of children and young people, through both illness and accident, which he found to be especially difficult to deal with professionally and personally.

'I cannot confess to finding words easy in those circumstances, despite having had to face it many times,' Arthur admitted. 'In the midst of grief and sorrow, there may also be anguish and guilt. "If only..." is the most common comment at a time like this.'

As he comforts a couple in their time of grief he knows also that he has a duty to assist the medical staff in discussing the matter of organ donation. If only they could wait until parents get over their initial grief; but this is impossible.

'It is so easy to sound coldly medical and talk of "giving life to someone else" when the centre of prayer and thought at that time is with the young life in front of you: but it has to be faced.'

Pastoral care in such situations may not end at the hospital door. For days, weeks and perhaps months after a funeral, the reality of bereavement is still there and the pain and recriminations are not buried with the coffin. Contact with parents may continue for some time and he is often touched by the things they say to him. The following is an extract from a letter written four months after a child's death from an accident in the home:

> I'd really like to believe that there is such a place as heaven where my wee boy now is and that some day I'll be with him again. Perhaps my faith will one day be stronger to find comfort in this belief. In the meantime, I thank you again for your prayers and counselling and hope that one day I'll meet you again.

'Theological training, books of sermons and other publications do not always help you to find the right words. Perhaps it is something to do with the fact that the Bible does not try to hide from the difficult aspects of life and death that I find words there. It speaks of and to real human beings.

'I learn from the Bible, not just how to develop my theology but to recognise how Christ ministered. He was on the spot at the time. He was not afraid to rejoice with those who rejoiced and to weep with those who mourned. He could not be everywhere at the same time and it is true that many were not touched by him. But today, the difference is that his Spirit is omnipresent.'

Faced with a search for words to say, Arthur often finds that he too wants to weep and cry to heaven, 'WHY, Lord?' He admits to being only marginally ahead of those he has been called to help as far as understanding is concerned. Perhaps it is because of this admission of his own uncertainties that they are able to be helped by him.

'I represent him and his hands and prayers in these situations - for there are no human answers - and I am the one who is there on his behalf. This is what makes this ministry so different - just being there is the challenge of the moment.'

In a report he had to do on his work to the Health Board, he suggested that the most important aspect of chaplaincy is 'being there' and he gave examples:

Being there when the amputation decision is irreversible. *Being there* when the favourable or unfavourable biopsy returns. *Being there* when you realise others with you have not survived the road accident, the hotel fire, the mountain fall. *Being there* when you realise you are going to walk again; talk again; work again; love again; live again.

There is no doubt that many people have been touched through the ministry of Arthur Fraser. Those who have met him in hospital speak highly of him and that also among the eighty per cent who have no church connection. He is greatly respected by, and works closely with, ministers throughout the Highlands and Islands. He contacts all of the churches whose members he has visited and may refer those who have shown an interest or become Christians.

With seriously ill patients, whose link with the church may be tenuous to say the least, he finds that they also need to be ministered to. He remembers in particular an old man who was not a regular attender at church. At death's door, he sought the chaplain's help. He was distressed and asked for communion to be given to him.

'Now this puts the whole subject of Communion on to a different plain. There are no communicants classes, no preparatory services, no fencing of the table. This man had not previously professed faith, yet he wanted to take bread and wine with me. There and then he

91

admitted his faith in Christ as his Saviour and Lord. I could not question the sincerity of his words, nor ask him to wait to find out if his faith worked out in practice when he attended a church.

'Whatever really happened on that occasion will be told in eternity but I do know that, when I prayed, he prayed and I have to admit that the old man was transformed from a fearful and tearful human being to one who was content and assured.'

The other side of the coin is illustrated by his account of a patient who had made life a misery for all of the staff. He was in great pain and had a terminal illness but his behaviour was as much a manifestation of the way he had lived to date, as it was a response to the pain he was enduring. Arthur did his best to intervene and built up a rapport, more as a fellow Glaswegian than as a man of the cloth. Arthur listened while the man recounted his life to him. He had been a hard man most of his life and his wife had left him, yet his workmates seemed to take a liking to his earthiness, nevertheless.

'Right, Arthur,' the man said, in a still broad Glasgow accent, 'I want you to take my funeral but none o' these lies that I was really a goody goody at heart and that the Lord is getting a good "yin". '

At his funeral, Arthur did just that; told those who attended that he had 'come to bury a self-confessed sinner and not a saint' and spoke to the mourners about the gospel, making no pious statements about the man's belief or destiny. After the service a number of his workmates thanked him for his honesty and confessed to being touched by his words.

Arthur pointed out, 'Some people like to think that

there will always be time for a deathbed conversion and that they can live as they like up to then. They may quote the story of the dying thief in support of their argument. While I recognise, in cases similar to the one I first described, that God is not limited to time and space in that he can intervene at the last moment, I believe that it is the exception. Christianity is about living more than dying and, the younger people are when they commit their life to Christ, the more they can do for him in this troubled world we live in.'

Fortunately, few teenagers are admitted to hospital, but Arthur finds it most rewarding to speak to them, enjoying their openness and realistic attitude to many aspects of life. 'I find that the, so called, macho ones and even the shy ones, sometimes open up to me when they are away from the pressures of home or peers. It is always a delight for me to refer them to a youth group in a local church or introduce them to a fellowship.'

Sometimes it is the committed Christian whose faith is challenged during their time in hospital or by the inevitability of death. The strictly brought up Highland Presbyterian, with long held quasi-Calvinistic views, can be faced with doubts and uncertainties which are hard to counteract.

'It is a phenomenon I did not meet quite so often before I came to the Highlands. The hymn *Blessed Assurance* is certainly not in the repertoire of many people I have met and it is disturbing for me to meet wonderfully committed Christians whose peace is destroyed by doubts and fears which reflect their upbringing more than their knowledge of the Bible. I am careful not to be dismissive of beliefs held by any denomination but try to read and pray with such people so that they can seek God's Word for themselves at that time.'

Just as difficult to deal with can be the Christian who has believed, or been told, that God will always intervene to save their life and that he will perform a miracle. Some are disappointed and recovery is not given, creating a tremendous turmoil of faith and disillusionment. They require tender and careful counselling. Arthur has seen many wonderful cases of recovery after prayer but he is quick to point out that all decisions about healing are in God's hands and that the medical services, and indeed the National Health Service, are also gifts which God has given to us for healing.

Aware that he had only briefly spoken about his own home and family I was keen to know how the demands of his work had affected this area of his life. He spoke of the wonderful prayerful support of his GP wife Marion, of her patience, of her being an ear to listen to his concerns and worries and, perhaps above all, of being a companion to relax and find recreation with when away from the demands of the chaplaincy. He has, in fact, a 24 hour job and can be on call at any time, although more recently the work is shared with a parttime associate chaplain.

'It is not easy when I have returned home tired, changed into relaxing clothes and am about to sit down to a nice quiet dinner with Marion when the phone rings. In our work it could be for either of us and we know that often there is no option but to go out.'

Family life with their children has meant a lot to them and has provided the base for the work which Arthur has done over the years in various ministries.

Now that they are grown up and away from home, he and Marion have more time to be together - that is, when the medical services allow it!

Their own lives have been challenged as they have experienced illness themselves. In particular, Arthur's emergency admission to hospital in 1989 with a cardiac problem, gave the family a great fright and put him into the position of patient for a change.

'I learned that I had a viral infection which affects the heart. The staff were great although they did have a good joke with me and made the most of the change of role. It does make me that bit more appreciative of the feeling of hopelessness and vulnerability which the bedridden patient may experience.'

When I first spoke to Arthur about including him in this book, he admitted to wondering what he had to contribute that was out of the ordinary. 'I don't see my life as having been any different from many other Christians,' he said, 'I have never seen myself as special at all.'

As he told me his story, however, it became clear to him that there were indeed events in his life which had come together in an interesting and ordered way. It is also true that God has used him to reach out and help others in the past and that, in his present post, as many of his hospital and church colleagues stress, he makes a vital contribution to that interrelated circle he outlines to the trainee nurses. Men and women are not simply flesh and blood but are indeed complex beings with a body, mind and spirit to be catered for.

Varied and challenging though his work is, Arthur Fraser sees himself as fulfilling the Lord's work as he speaks to people at their bedside, comforts the bereaved or shares in the joy of new found health. He humbly maintains that he is simply reflecting a verse, which he quoted to me more than once, 'When I was sick you visited me.'

5
A Sense of Direction

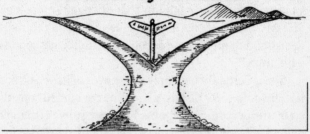

'...and, Joy, I need a decision within the hour, come what may!'

The concluding words of the Managing Director at headquarters were still ringing in her ears as she made her way from her office to the board room to meet with her managers that Monday morning. Several thousand pounds worth of business might be gained or lost, depending on her decision.

For Joy Mackenzie, Director and General Manager of an Aberdeen company, her life now is a far cry from her childhood days on the family croft in the Highlands, when the greatest decision she had to make was whether to milk the cow before or after breakfast. Then she would go happily off to school on the bus without a care in the world. In those days Mum and Dad shouldered the responsibility of running home and business.

But the buck stopped with her now. As she considered the various options open to her, she recalled the words of a colleague, said perhaps more in jest than out of respect for her beliefs, 'You have an advantage over all of us when it comes to making decisions, Joy. You can pray about it!' He may have been teasing her then, but it is just what she found herself doing that morning - in her mind, quietly and unceremoniously.

'It must have been the fastest prayer I have ever made - so fast, in fact, that it couldn't have been any more than "Help!" I do feel that I was guided to make the right decision, although, some people might think that sounds a bit crazy.'

She is certainly not crazy in the eyes of her boss, nor her customers, for that matter, as she has gained considerable respect since she joined the company. Turnover under her leadership has more than doubled. At any one time she leads a workforce of between eighty and a hundred people with four managers under her.

'I have no doubt in my mind that I could not do anything without God's help,' she argued. 'My Christian life is central to all that I do and believe.'

Despite her success in business to date, she is unassuming in the way she presents herself and insists that she has never really been an ambitious person.

'I see ruthless ambition in so many people that I do not wish to emulate them. Yes, I am ambitious - but for my company, not openly for myself. I believe that I have a duty to do my best for my employers, with all the strength and ability that God has given me. But this should apply to any Christian employee - or employer, when you think of it.'

Still only 'thirtysomething' she has, nevertheless, had a fairly meteoric career to date. As she mapped out her life from her early days in Gairloch, we talked at length about her faith, the challenges to it and the sense of direction which she now realises God has given her.

Although brought up in a Christian home, her sentiments were not always so positive. Along with other youngsters from remote communities, she left home after primary school, to live in the county town of Dingwall to receive her secondary education. She rebelled against the numerous, seemingly meaningless, rules and regulations with which hostel life was riddled. Things like, 'You don't polish your shoes in the cloakroom because common sense tells you that you don't do that.' Or, even more incredible, 'If you don't eat all the food on your plate, you will have to report to Mr MacNab.' In fact, it was doubtful whether the said gentleman, Depute Director of Education at the time, was really interested whether or not the girls finished their cornflakes in the morning!

'There were hundreds of *rules* like that which we used to joke about, and I have to confess I was not the most respectful of that type of authority. Along with my compatriots I was frequently found in the kitchens doing the dishes - the popular punishment. I often think that the Council must have saved a fortune in staff wages for dishwashing during our days in hostel! I suppose in many ways we deserved it, but it has given me an inbuilt suspicion of "rules" unless I can clearly see the meaning and purpose of them.'

Joy was quite glad, therefore, to go to college in Aberdeen, to lodgings where life was more free and easy. She was still a bit homesick, even although she had already lived away from home for several years. But her sister also lived in The Granite City at the time and she took her along to church. She also introduced the young student to her friends who were really kind and welcoming.

'I was, however, enjoying life; and religion did not seem to fit my idea of enjoyment. I did feel that I would like to be a Christian one day, but later, perhaps, after I had done all I wanted to do. Yes, maybe when I was about 70 - just before I would die. At least, that is what I thought. I suppose you could say that God had other plans. He often does, doesn't he?"

Her parents, her sisters and many other friends, caring about the direction she was taking in her life, were praying for her. She knows that some of her friends at school and college did indeed make a mess of their lives in the 'rebellious seventies', but at that time she was far from caring.

One Christmas she went home as usual, looking forward to seeing her folks but not to hearing the customary long sermons. But to church she went, dutifully. The preaching of her minister spoke directly to her.

'*Boast not thyself of tomorrow, for you know not what a day may bring forth* was the text that was brought home to me. As far as I was concerned, I wanted to live for today. Tomorrow would take care of itself. Yet I knew what I should do. I knew in whom I should trust. What if I don't live long enough to do all that I want to do? Such thoughts raced through my mind that night and I made up my mind to follow the same Jesus whom I had heard so much about from my mother's knee.'

After college, she joined the bank near her home, to the delight of her parents. They were pleased to have her back at the family croft for a while.

'These were months of growing and settling down in the faith, building on what I had been taught in my youth. Yet I still felt that there was perhaps a bigger world out there for me to see, in both my professional and my Christian life,' she recalled.

She was not too unhappy, therefore, to leave home once again when the bank transferred her to Aberdeen. Unlike the last time she made her way to the big city, on this occasion she made a point of seeking friendship and fellowship with other Christians. In due course she settled within the fellowship of Gilcomston South Church of Scotland, which has not only been a place to worship on Sundays but has also become her spiritual home in Aberdeen.

'A sort of haven,' she says, 'where I can be refreshed and replenished physically and spiritually at the end of a busy week. I also appreciate greatly the ministry of the Rev. William Still.'

Her business life took a new turn when she was appointed secretary to the managing director of an old established horticultural firm. She enjoyed working there and was given considerable responsibility.

When the company was taken over in 1985 she wondered what her future would be. She was to find out sooner than she expected when her boss called her into his office one morning.

Picking up her notebook from the desk as usual, she prepared to take a letter for him. He asked her to sit down as she lifted her pencil in readiness. But instead of giving her a name and address for the letterhead, he asked a question that was to lead to a turning point in her life, 'We're looking for someone to run the company, Joy. Will you do it?'

It's not every day that the boss offers his chair to his

secretary, except perhaps in deference to her gender, when all other seats in the room have been taken! Certainly, she knew the job. She understood how the company worked on a day-to-day basis. But in a decision making situation - with thousands of pounds to win or lose ...? The surprise must have shown in her face.

'You might want some time to think about it.'

'I would indeed,' she replied, with more than a little hesitation.

'Well, let me know - as soon as possible,' he continued, as she rose to leave.

Her head was still reeling when she left the managing director's office and she can't remember much about the rest of the day other than that she thought and, certainly, prayed a lot about the unexpected offer. She recalled the turmoil in her mind.

'The decision was not easy. One minute I was persuading myself that I could do it, the next I was plagued with doubts. How would the office staff react? The other managers? The customers? Would I have the confidence to make decisions and carry them out?'

Uppermost in her mind was one hard fact of business life. Despite 'equal opportunities' being the order of the day, the reality is that we live in a man's world! Could she cope with all the challenges, wheeling and dealing which her male colleagues appeared to take in their stride? Would she be able to avoid the 'rat race', the stress and the strain of struggling from one sales figure to the next? The same pressures which pushes many businessmen to an early grave?

'It may seem strange now, but the question of money did not enter into my head. Yes, of course, everyone thinks of that when considering promotion. But I hadn't considered promotion. I did not apply for a job, as I had done when I joined the company. It was being offered to me - on a plate, as it were.'

It was then she appreciated the opportunity to confide in her close friends and relatives; not just for sound advice, humanly speaking, but also for their support and prayer in making a decision from a Christian standpoint.

After much heart-searching, she decided to take on the job, not because she was bursting with ambition and confidence, but because she believed that the abilities and experience which God allowed her to have should be put to use; a viewpoint surely alien to most jobseekers in the cut-throat world of business today. Had she thought about it, she would have found precedents in the Bible. One could mention Joseph, Moses, Esther, Nehemiah or Daniel, all of whom found themselves in positions, not exactly of their own choosing, because God wanted them there. In fact, it was a series of sermons on Daniel, referring to this very point, which helped her with one of many dilemmas she was to face in her business life.

Early on she knew that she would have to make a decision about her involvement on Sundays, when 25% of the company's business is achieved. It was so important to her that she brought it up before accepting the promotion, firmly believing that her stance would be viewed as restrictive to her effective performance and that it would lose her the position.

To her amazement, the group chairman showed no hesitation when he confirmed his offer to her. He trusted his own judgment and put her in place immediately. Not surprisingly, two years later, when turnover had increased dramatically with his protegee at the helm, he made her a director of the company.

'I suppose the issue of Sunday trading in the business will always be at the back of my mind. It is one thing to enjoy a relaxing visit to a garden centre on a Sunday afternoon; many of my Christian friends do that. It is quite another thing to be the director of the operation, where your main purpose and motivation is to make money. That, I believe, is the dilemma for a Christian in my position.

'On odd occasions I can be called out when emergencies arise and I believe that it is correct for me to do so. The stories of Daniel and others keep coming back to me. He was working in a situation which could cause godly people to raise their eyebrows - what's a nice person like him doing in a place like that? I could sum it up succinctly with the motto, *Bloom Where You Are Planted*, if you will forgive the horticultural pun!'

We all like to be popular and feel that our colleagues enjoy being with us. Joy got on well with the office staff when she was a secretary. But her sudden elevation to a position of authority surprised many of them and affected her relationship with some of them. She is unsure to this day if it was just their failure to accept that she could effectively fill the shoes of an established and well respected manager.

'It was one of the hardest times in my life. People whom I thought I could work with, turned against me and I began to realise that it was going to be tough. But something inside me - my faith and, yes, a good bit of

Highland determination - made me want to carry it through, come what may. I wanted to prove to myself, as well as to others, that I could do it.'

The management were very supportive and even allowed one or two to resign who would not accept her position. Joy acknowledges that, had it not been for the support of her family and friends, one of the most difficult times she has experienced could have had an adverse effect on her health, mentally and physically.

'It certainly was quite a baptism. I got to know the people at the Conciliatory and Arbitration Service (ACAS) very well indeed. Even they said, "It has been tough for you." But, at the time, I was aware that I was given the strength to go in to the office every day. I am in no doubt that God helped me. The support of many friends in the church and at work was invaluable during that period of my life.'

Reading the letters of Peter helped her a lot. There she learned how the apostle, once humbled, found that God supported and guided him to enable him to carry on. In turn, his letters to the Early Church were used by God to support it at a time of growth, challenge and persecution. She came to realise that on occasion God allows us to go through trials. From a position of weakness, we may appreciate his strength all the more, and look more positively at our experience.

Without doubt, Joy has found strengthen from those events, both as a Christian and a businesswoman. Traumatic though it was, it proved to be an excellent training experience, preparing her for the reality of the job that had been entrusted to her.

Too often the media announce yet another example

of corruption in the world of commerce. Joy is very aware of the temptations which confront people in business. On more than one occasion her own integrity has been put to the test.

She remembers when one of her managers expressed concern about a large contract that was being negotiated with a company. All was going well until the representative dropped a strong hint that he expected some private work to be 'quietly' included in the cost. Joy was consulted and, having thought it through, the management team agreed they would not allow it. They kept the contract but the customer did not return with further business.

'I am pleased to say that the senior directors and local management have always backed me in such decisions, despite the potential loss of business and the real, or imagined, effect on customer relations. Business integrity is so important and very often it is not clear-cut and dried - it is a measured judgment. Christian character displayed in facing these decisions is much more effective than 'mouthing' about one's faith to colleagues. I don't believe the Christian life to be mushy or sentimental. It is about day-to-day issues.

'Sadly, I know only too well that many Christian employees in other companies are regularly faced with potentially compromising situations and it cannot be easy for them.'

If only the issues of morality were black and white, life would be so much easier - or would it? More often than not, it is the 'grey' areas which provide us with the greatest challenge to our faith. There is the danger that we try to raise ourselves to a spiritual plain, where we think we have all the answers. We might call it 'guidance' but we are in danger of overlooking our own humanity, with its many pitfalls.

'My fear, when agreeing to be included in a book like this,' Joy continued, 'is that I will appear to be saying that all one needs to do is trust and have faith that all will go well in the end. And I worry that I might make a mistake one day, make a wrong decision and fall, thereby undoing all that I have tried to do and be in my life. I do have to keep reminding myself of God's promise that he will keep us. That is very comforting.'

Time and time again, she stressed the importance of realising that God is not in the business of making us 'superhuman'. However, he can help us to make the most of the talents that he has given us. She spoke of the need to walk with God ('chatting' to him in the course of the day, she put it), to get to know his will, by reading the Bible, praying and having fellowship with others.

'I feel very, very human most of the time - especially on a Monday morning or when other people are getting under my skin. But I believe that the suppression of my natural responses is as much a reflection of my training as it is of my faith. If I did not believe that, I would not take part in expensive training programmes for my staff. It is not biblical to say "trust in God and you'll do your job well" nor is it good business practice!'

Being a Christian is not a passport to an easy life, she underlined. Elaborating on this theme, she spoke of a number of difficult situations she has faced. On one occasion, she was called out to deal with an alleged case of dishonesty with one of the staff. After lengthy interviews with the accused and witnesses, the employee eventually asked to see Joy in private to confess to what had happened.

'Although I had no alternative but dismissal, I also made the difficult decision not to press charges, realising that this may be against general company policy. I suppose I wanted to temper judgment with mercy but I also realised that the employee's family had been devastated by the whole affair. In addition, I believed there had been pressure from friends resulting in this uncharacteristic behaviour. I make up my mind about things often because I feel that it is right for me at the time not because someone else has suggested it. Our senior directors at head office supported my decision.'

It is difficult for any of us not to respond to a tug at the heartstrings and some say that it is easier for a man than a woman to be hard and uncompromising in business. When one is responsible for the training and monitoring of the performance of others, there will inevitably be honest but hard words to deliver. One of the difficult things to do is to tell a member of staff that his or her work is not up to standard and that the company no longer wishes to employ them. Joy has had to do this from time to time.

'Perhaps the worst occasion for me was when one of my managers consistently failed to do the job properly. I knew him so well and liked him very much as a person but I was also aware that we had to continue to gain business and make a profit or no employee's job would be safe. To have to sit with him that afternoon and tell him that his future depended on his performance, really tugged at my heartstrings. But it is a job I am expected to do and, although it is always painful, one tries to display care for the individual, balanced with necessary firmness.'

As Joy suspected, she has had an uphill struggle to convince some people that she can do the job. It has been more to do with her response to the challenge of being female in a man's world than about her qualifications and experience. Most men admit to finding it 'interesting' to deal with an attractive woman and many businesses may take advantage of this on the sales front. Did Joy ever consider that she was being 'used' in this way?

'No I can't say that has ever been a worry,' she replied, laughing. 'I think men are now beginning to realise that a businesswoman is there to do business, not to be chatted up in a patronising way. If I become aware of an awkwardness with someone, I find it helpful to keep the conversation very task-orientated and concentrate on being objective about the job in hand. This usually eases any tension and overcomes the problem.

'Of course, I am no less human than anyone else and I sometimes feel vulnerable. I am attracted to some men - and not to others! Christians are no different from anyone else in this respect but we have a responsibility to live up to our Christian principles. There is a bonus, I think, of living under the canopy of God's love. You are part of a family and a fellowship that cares for you prayerfully. I am sure we are often steered away from danger and from situations which would be unhelpful to us by God keeping his eye on us, even when we do not particularly ask him for guidance.

'I find that reassuring when I am rushing around making quick, possibly rash, decisions. I have personally been aware of this protection more than once. I recall in particular one occasion when I was perhaps becoming too involved in a relationship which was not beneficial and I felt I was helped to deal with a very difficult situation. Sometime later a friend told me that, without knowing my circumstances at all, she had felt led to pray for me a lot during that period. I do not believe that was coincidental.'

Working 60 hours a week, on call virtually 24 hours a day to deal with emergency situations, Joy certainly does lead a very busy life and she is aware now that there was a time when she was in danger of joining the ranks of the 'workaholics'. She speaks openly and in an animated way about the range of responsibilities she has. Single and unattached, with no pressing family responsibilities, it would be so easy for her to live, work and sleep on a job which she enjoys so much.

The trap which so many people in business fall into is that they devote more and more time to their work than they do to friends, family and, above all their spiritual life.

At a time when this may have been the direction she was taking, she was due to have a meeting with one of her fellow directors. En route to Aberdeen in his car, he became so unwell that he diverted to hospital in Dundee to seek assistance. The phone call later in the evening, informing her that he had died that afternoon of a massive heart attack, left her numb.

'I could not take it in. This was the first time I had been faced with the death of someone close to me. I just could not believe that he would not be in the office the next day, nor ever again. The finality of it shook me to the core. I knew that he spent a lot more time in business than in leisure and that he was very much under stress; a classic example of a 'workaholic'. For some reason, I felt guilty but, above all I realised that we were both young directors in the company. He was only thirty-five when he died, leaving a young wife, whom I knew so well. They had welcomed me to their home on many occasions.

'At his funeral I thought I might be the strong one but it didn't work out that way. I went to pieces and did not have the words to say. When the minister conducting the funeral referred to my colleague attending church, that also hit me. I have to confess that I was unaware of any interest he may have had in spiritual things and I wondered whether he knew of my faith.'

When she travelled to Glasgow to help sort out the business affairs of the young director, she found herself plagued with fatigue and stress and the question going round and round in her head, 'Could that have been me?' She began to lose concentration as she worked hard between the two jobs.

'I think I realised then the danger of overworking and becoming too absorbed in my occupation. I have learned so much from that time. I took a week off work and went home to Gairloch where I believe God spoke very clearly to me. I learned to get my priorities right, to put the whole scene into perspective. It was not simply a matter of spending less time at work but knowing when to find time to relax physically and be renewed spiritually. God has given us a mind and a body to use in his service and it is up to us to keep them in good order.'

Through this experience God taught her to be more

relaxed in her approach to the business. She knew then, if she did not know before, that to succeed in business was not the be all and the end all and that there were physical limits she must recognise.

'God also sets limits. I thought myself young and capable and was going round feeling that I could run the world. I had to learn to stop, look and listen. I had to take more time to be with others and with God. Putting things into perspective, and learning to slow down, helped me to work more effectively. I suppose it is the sort of thing you might read in any book on the subject of stress but I did not take time to find one. It took a dramatic experience like the death of a colleague to get the message home to me.'

Joy finds that many positive things from her Presbyterian background are now a strength to her. The need to persevere, to stand up for one's beliefs, not being the least of them. But in business and personal life an austere Highland upbringing can also have a negative effect.

'The God of my childhood was a Judge with a big stick, someone to fear and perhaps keep at a distance. As an adult I have learned more of a God who loves his people, who is not there to punish and banish his children but to love, guide and provide for them. Psalm 37 says, *Although we fall he is there with his right hand to pick us up*. The sort of thing a loving father does when his child stumbles on a path.

'His love is broader and wider than we can understand. He doesn't want to put us down or beat us into submission. He wants us to get up and get on with our Christian life. It is well known that the Highland culture can go hand in hand with a bit of an inferiority or guilt complex. If things are going well, something must be wrong in God's eyes.'

Joy confesses that she was really scared of God at one time. However, years of biblical teaching, in the atmosphere of love and fellowship that she has found in her present church, have enabled her to make sense spiritually of many of the things she knew about intellectually.

'The meaning of assurance is hard to define but I do know that I could not go out and do a day's work if I did not feel that God was with me. It does give a wonderful sense of security, which I believe is unique to Christians. It is hard for others to understand this. The lines of the hymn sums it up for me:

> The love of Jesus, what it is,
> None but his loved ones know...

Of course, my experience, my training, my knowledge of the company all play their part, but that is not enough to enable me to survive. I hear of so many people who turn to drink or something else to help them through the day, or night. I suppose I'm different in that I turn to the Bible - day and night!'

Joy particularly appreciates the meeting for prayer and fellowship she attends on a Saturday night, but she has also learned the importance of knowing how and when to relax, to look after herself physically. She plays squash twice a week, enjoys entertaining friends in her home and loves to get away from it all from time to time. She enjoys driving over to Gairloch to be with her family, sharing in the simplicity, and at times hard graft of crofting. But escaping is not always easy as she realised one Hogmanay, when the phone rang at 2 am.

' "Its for you, Joy. Someone from your office," my sister said when she woke me up. A burglar alarm had gone off in the middle of the night and no one could be contacted locally to give permission to disconnect it over the holiday period. Fortunately, nothing was stolen after my decision to let them go ahead! But part of my job is to be available and contactable almost always, and I accept that.'

If the delights of home at Gairloch are too far away for a short break, she appreciates the opportunity to spend a couple of days with a friend in one of the many charming little fishing ports within easy reach of Aberdeen.

Although more absorbed at present in her career than in thoughts of marriage and children of her own, Joy is always delighted to be with her sisters' families, ranging from a toddler to a ten year old.

'The children are great, and I love weekends and holidays with them. We have great fun sometimes when I take them on their own and allow them all the normally forbidden treats. In the Summer we usually manage some time together as a family in Gairloch and this is always very special. When the weather is nice we have a super time barbecuing on the shore, walking in the hills, playing crazy games till late at night and generally letting off steam. You can do all that with children in such an unselfconscious way, don't you think? And its very rejuvenating!'

We talked for a while about various attitudes to money and possessions, particularly in Christian circles. I asked Joy if she ever was made to feel uncomfortable by prospering when others may be struggling to make ends meet.

'People often ask me how right is it to work only for the purpose of making money and prospering. I suppose it is easy to be comfortable with money if you are on a good salary but, nevertheless, I believe that it is given to us in trust by God. Of course, we all have a responsibility to support the work of the church. I would be failing if I lost sight of that perspective but, yes, I enjoy buying good clothes, nice things for my home and going on holiday. They are part of me and give me the opportunity to relax and unwind. I believe that God enjoys prospering his people and he wants us to enjoy his blessings.

'One of my favourite hymns, in this context, is *When all thy mercies O my God* and, in particular, the lines:

Ten thousand, thousand precious gifts,
My daily thanks employ;
Nor is the least a cheerful heart,
That tastes those gifts with joy.

And, no, I did not realise that I appeared in the last line!'

It has been said that life can be lonely at the top, but clearly this is not the case for Joy. She is, nevertheless, quite far up the ladder and still young. Where does she go from here?

'I will remain in my job as long as I feel that it is God's place for me to be. Yes, I suppose that does sound a bit trite but I am confident that, whatever the future holds, it will be what God considers best for me, as is the case for all his children. My prayer is that I will be open to his leading and that, whatever the circumstances, I will stick close to him to serve him. Can I quote another hymn?

> Thee may our tongues for ever bless,
> Thee may we love alone,
> And ever in our lives express,
> The image of thine own.

That sums it all up for me. It is, I believe, the way to attain a healthy contentment and fulfilment which is I suppose what we all want.'

In an interview reported in a daily newspaper it was said that Joy's success in business has certainly resulted in many changes in her lifestyle. But it is a fitting, if unwitting, tribute to her beliefs and her faith that the writer of her profile concluded, 'Her lifestyle may have changed somewhat - but she has not.'

6
Worth the Risk

The 747 touched down smoothly at Nairobi airport, only a few minutes late. As he stepped from the air-conditioned interior of the plane, the stifling African heat caught his breath for a few seconds and he was momentarily dazzled by the bright sunlight. It had been a rather long, weary journey from London and he was looking forward to having a shower, a change of clothes and a quick nap at the hotel before meeting his hosts. But first, luggage had to be claimed and Customs cleared.

The bustling arrivals hall seemed only a few degrees cooler than outside on the tarmac, but he was glad to be out of the blazing sun as he made his way to the luggage carousel indicated for his flight number. Within a few minutes it whirred into life and the mass of perspiring passengers surged forward to peer at the first couple of cases which dropped on to it. Soon an assortment of baggage filled the conveyor belt, which clicked and thumped its way round the crowded circle of impatient travellers.

Gordon had travelled too often to allow himself to be caught up in the maelstrom of baggage claim areas, which so many voyagers seemed to revel in all over the world. He stood patiently at a good vantage point keeping a sharp eye for his case to fall onto the belt. He knew that he would recognise it immediately and was poised to move forward to an appropriate gap in the crowd to grasp hold of it.

He was a little disconcerted, however, when the squeaking carousel, now conveying only a couple of battered brown suitcases and a few airline courier bags, shuddered to an abrupt halt. The international traveller's greatest nightmare had become a reality. His luggage had gone missing - along with the clothes he was desperate to change into after the long journey.

After explanations to customs officials, he passed through the gate to be greeted warmly by the Kenyan who would be his guide during his stay.

'Just leave it to me, Professor Dickson,' he smiled broadly, as if he located lost luggage on a daily basis, when Gordon explained his predicament.

Despite exhaustive enquiries there was no trace of his luggage and no idea of its whereabouts. It is a risk we all take every time we fly and this was not the first time it had happened to Gordon Dickson, of all things, a Professor of Risk Management!

'They assure me that they will send it to you, Professor. Never fear, let us get some clothes for you.'

'We set off into town in his car through hectic traffic,' Gordon explained. 'I soon realised that there was no local Marks and Spencer to pop into and purchase a few necessities to tide me over. I was taken to a rather old-fashioned, but upmarket by Kenyan standards, menswear shop where the owner tried to charge me exorbitant prices. I appeared to him as a gullible foreigner ripe for the picking. Desperate to get out, have a shower and change into fresh clothing, I might have paid anything. "Yes, that's fine," I said, reaching for my wallet. My faithful guide muttered something to the merchant and covered my wallet with his hand. "That is only a quote, Professor. Too dear by far; you must haggle in Kenya."

'I managed to get an outfit at a greatly reduced price and smiled to myself when the thought crossed my mind of trying to bargain in a similar way in one of the major chains at home. My luggage did reach me, but not for a long time afterwards.'

Many of us would have despaired and been flustered in such a situation, but Gordon Dickson has learned to take such incidents in his stride. As the only professor in his field in the United Kingdom and a renowned author on the subject, his expertise is much sought after throughout Great Britain and the world. He is a seasoned traveller, acutely aware of the risks he takes when flying around the globe.

Some years ago, Gordon would not have had the faintest vision of such an experience, and certainly not in the heat of Africa. Not madly ambitious in his school days, he would not have aspired to such worldwide recognition even if he had been aware that a subject such as 'Risk Management' existed at all.

People who meet the much sought after lecturer 'off-stage', as it were, realise quickly that he does not fit into the oft painted picture of the international go-getter and jet-setter, typical in the hustle and bustle of business life today.

Although dedicated to the work he does from his British base, it is only one dimension to his life. The others he would confess to being more central and just as time consuming; namely, his church and family life with his wife, Moira and two teenage daughters, Julie and Jennifer.

'I enjoy my job immensely, although there is not as much glamour to international travel as some might imagine. But central to my life is my faith, my family and Christian work.'

Brought up on the outskirts of a large Scottish city, his early years were peppered with more than a few challenges. Even on the day he was born - he was delivered at home - he had to be rushed to hospital when his leg was found to be broken at birth. When only a year old he developed a mysterious illness which caused concern and resulted in a rapid deterioration in his health. Only massive doses of the then new drug Penicillin led to his eventual recovery.

A rather uneventful few years at primary school followed, where he does not feel he excelled himself academically. These were days when primary pupils had to pass entrance exams if they wished to pursue an academic education.

'Where I lived, the primary school did not seem to have a very big quota for the Academy and, no matter how well you thought you had done, it was difficult to get there. I ended up attending the Junior Secondary school, much to the concern of my parents who had greater ambitions for me.'

His father was a fairly quiet, unassuming man who would not have normally wished to stir up trouble.

However, he wrote to the Director of Education to ask for his son to be transferred to an academic course.

'In retrospect, I now realise how important this uncharacteristic action of my father was in shaping my future career, and perhaps my spiritual life. I did feel out of place in the junior school, where I was taught to believe that I might not be capable of anything. I may have embarked on an unfulfilling educational and professional career had it not been for his perseverance. I would venture to say now that it was very much part of God's plan for my life.'

Despite the success of his father's action, Gordon found a certain stigma attached to the lower F class to which he was allocated. This was reflected in the attitude of other children who had not 'missed a year' and in some teachers who treated them less favourably than their A pupils.

'At the risk of sounding political, it has made me grateful that my own children have not had to face selection at such a crucial stage in their lives, despite the criticisms from certain quarters of the system we enjoy at present. I feel that it is invidious to decide the future of a child at such a formative age,' Gordon expressed forcibly.

He persevered and worked hard to continue for a sixth year at school. It was only during the last couple of years, however, that his self-confidence was boosted as he achieved success in exams, assisted by a few dedicated teachers who recognised his ability and encouraged him to achieve his full potential.

'In my sixth year, there was a big decision to make. What do I do with my life, career wise? But a year before that, a more important decision had to be made, which would affect my spiritual well-being.'

Gordon had chosen to take economics as a subject. During his fifth year a young, newly trained teacher joined the staff; she was to prove to be an important influence in his life.

'She was an attractive person and a good teacher but I am afraid the fifth year boys, myself included, plagued her life every week. There was nothing vicious or violent, just down right bad behaviour in class. She was not from our part of the country so this included making fun of her accent,' Gordon confessed.

When she called him out and asked him to wait behind in class one day, he was sure that he was in for some trouble this time round. Neither corporal punishment nor a few hundred lines awaited him, however. She spoke to him for a while and then, seemingly out of the blue, asked, 'Gordon, why don't you come and join a Church Summer Mission Team that I am leading?'

'I do not know yet what she was thinking, or what she saw in me to even consider asking me to do such a thing for, of all of the boys in the class I was perhaps the most unlikely one to respond to her invitation. More for a dare and a laugh, I suppose, I agreed to go; although I still cannot understand why. In retrospect, however, I see this also as part of some plan that God had for me.'

The adventure, a 'big joke' to his friends, was to be a turning point in his life. As he worked with children and young people in a small Scottish town, alongside a group of dedicated Christian leaders, he soon wanted to find out what they had in their lives that made them want to tell others about it. The Bible in general, and the gospel of Christ in particular, became alive to him for the first time.

As his parents were regular church goers and members of the local congregation, he faithfully attended Sunday School. As an active member of the Boys' Brigade also, it was a story he had heard before. But, on this occasion, he was made more aware of the demands of the Christian life and, above all, he knew that he was certainly not following it. Already beginning to drift away from church, he now knew that he had to decide which path he was going to take in his spiritual life.

'The message of the minister who led it, and the dedication of the team, persuaded me to ask Christ to come into my life, to help me to live in the way that I had heard so much about and that had been offered so openly to me.

'That experience has also shaped my attitude to the Summer Mission work in which I am now involved. The Christian qualities of the leader, and the influence that a dedicated team can have on each other and on those whom they address in mission, are crucial. Somehow, God works through our words and our actions. Other people may be drawn to Christ or repelled from him by who we are and what we do. These issues play a central part in the training we give to the young folk who join us today.'

The economics teacher who boldly asked one of her troublesome pupils to join a mission team was one of the first to see the change in his life for, during his final year at school, he began to attend the 'Seekers Club' which she had organised after classes for interested teenagers.

'If there is any hidden educational message in this whole saga of my school career, it is that teachers, above all Christian teachers, should never underestimate the influence that they have on the moral and spiritual life of their pupils by the things they do and say to them.'

As a more committed church member, Gordon found himself, as many overenthusiastic young Christians do, beginning to 'compartmentalise' the Sunday School teachers and Boys' Brigade leaders according to the commitment that he perceived they portrayed. This did not really help him to fit into the work there.

'Eventually, as I matured in the faith, I came to accept everyone for the gifts they had, while at the same time recognising that some were more or less committed than I was.

'The most marked change in my life was in the Boys' Brigade, which I had attended faithfully for many years, mainly, I have to confess, because I play the bagpipes, and had an opportunity to develop my skills and perform in public in the band. When I came back from the mission that year, however, playing the bagpipes took second place to my attendance at, and my eventual leadership of, the Bible Class. The whole focus of my work in the Brigade changed.'

Having taken this crucial decision in his life at a time when he would soon choose a career, like many similarly committed young people, he was challenged by the thought of going into full-time Christian work. He wrestled with this for some time and reached the point of applying for selection school for the ministry. When he was offered a place at St. Andrew's University to study divinity this seemed to be confirmation that God was leading him in that direction.

'Then, for reasons I cannot explain, for I certainly did not hear a voice or anything like that, I decided that this was not the path that I should follow and turned down a much sought after place at one of Scotland's top universities. To the surprise of many of my friends and relatives, I left school and got a job in an insurance office.'

He continued to study and soon qualified as a Fellow of the Chartered Insurance Institute. Despite his success and the challenging and interesting position he held, he felt unfulfilled working in this sector. An opportunity arose at a local college to do some part-time teaching of his subject in evening classes. When a vacancy came up for a full-time post, he applied and was offered the job.

'When I look back on my career it was a bit like a pinball machine, with my life shooting about all over the place from one thing to another. I had been interviewed in different parts of the country for various jobs and had even been offered places elsewhere while I waited to hear from the college.

'I often wonder what direction my life might have taken had I gone for this job or that. Of course, dear to me now, more perhaps than in my youth, is my consciousness of God's purpose and plan for my life. If we commit our lives to Christ we must believe that, but it does not absolve us of the responsibility to play our part in reaching our full potential, educationally and otherwise.'

Service with the Boys' Brigade continued in the meantime and a further key influence in his life came on to the scene in the form of a new Captain. Attendance had declined and the work was struggling in the face of other attractions for teenagers.

'The new Captain, a well built and commanding figure, took the place by storm,' Gordon recalled. 'On the first night he addressed the dwindling group of boys from the platform at the end of the hall, in a loud and authoritative voice. "I'm here to tell you about Jesus. If you don't want to hear about Jesus, stand over there." And he pointed to the far wall. Nobody moved. It may sound drastic and off-putting in today's climate of opinion but, two years later, attendance had increased to over a hundred.

'If I needed to be convinced of anything, this experience showed me that teenagers don't want anything watered down. They don't want any simple, diluted story about Jesus or to be led into believing other than the facts of the gospel. They do not require the message to be so embellished that it cannot be recognised: of course, it should be well presented, interesting and appropriate to their life and times. Our boys were more keen to attend a well structured Bible Class than many other leaders before him had believed when they used various other means to attract them.'

The Bible Class continued for many years to be the main church activity for him. Under the effective leadership of the Captain he was to learn much of what he now puts into practice in his youth work today.

'I owe so much to the example he showed in dealing with the oldest and the roughest of youths who attended. I learned that it is possible to be caring and loving while at the same time setting down rules and limits which must be obeyed for the benefit of all. Discipline is perhaps not a popular word, much to the chagrin of teachers and youth workers. But it is, I believe, central to good order in all walks of life and there is no exception within church work. I believe too that the great majority of youngsters actually accept it and would thrive on it if it were more openly practised in family and community life.'

Church activities and lecturing did not take up all of his waking hours, for during this time he met up with Moira, whom he had known briefly during his primary school days. 'I think my first encounter with her,' he added wryly, 'was when I let down the tyres of her bicycle (an alternative then to pulling her pigtails) when I was ten years old!'

She must have forgiven him for they got married and moved to live in another part of Glasgow from where they had been brought up. They continued to travel across town to their former church but, after their daughters were born, joined their local congregation at Greenbank Church which was to become their spiritual home and a base for Christian work at home and in different parts of the country in later years.

Gordon led the Bible Class there for ten years, building on the experience he had gained under his former Boys' Brigade Captain, before eventually taking over the leadership of the large Sunday School and becoming an elder. Remembering his days on mission and the turning point that it had been in his own life, he felt that many of the teenagers in the church would benefit from working together as a team in a similar way.

'I became aware that many of them found it difficult

to deepen and enrich their new found faith unless they had an outlet in Christian work. While so often we criticise the aimlessness of teenagers today, we also underestimate them and are reluctant to give them responsibility both in and out of the church. This may be visiting the old folk in the congregation, cutting grass, giving out hymn books, helping in the Sunday School, to mention but a few.

'Summer Mission also seemed to me to be one way that we could be of help to them in this respect, so I applied to organise and lead one of the many outreaches to towns and villages which take place every year throughout our country. We were offered either a large coastal city or a small rural seaside town in the North of Scotland and we chose the latter.

'We have been taking young people to the attractive cathedral town of Dornoch since the Summer of 1984, where we organise activities for children and young people, locals and holidaymakers. With the support of members of the local churches, we trust that, over the years, we have been able to be a positive influence among the young people we meet. It is our prayer, of course, that through the songs, sketches and workshops that they will also get to know more about the Bible and become familiar with the meaning of the gospel of Christ. We have been encouraged to meet the same children year after year, some of whom are now teenagers who help us and work with us from time to time.'

As he had hoped, the work of Summer Mission, has indeed enriched the life of the young people in Greenbank and it is now an important dimension to the life of their church.

In the meantime, Gordon's career was moving forward as rapidly as his family and church life. Although he enjoyed lecturing in insurance, and had a professional qualification, lurking at the back of his mind somewhere was the feeling that he had lost out in some way by not taking up the chance of a university education. Being a young academic, he had some time to think things through and to develop his career; indeed, he was encouraged to do so by the college. He decided to study for a Masters Degree as a part-time research student.

'I started work on the study of Decision Making and Management and after a year I was registered as a Master of Literature, by research. I pursued that for three years and eventually graduated. That whetted my appetite for study so I decided to go on to do a PhD on Attitudes to Risk. This was also on a part-time basis with the support, not only of the college but also of my wife who had to run house and home while I spent many of my evenings poring over books and research documents and writing essays.'

After a further three years, he graduated PhD. Looking back, he now values the self-discipline which resulted from the need to order his time and study while simultaneously maintaining his family and church life.

He progressed to become Senior Lecturer, Reader and, when the opportunity arose, their first Professor of Risk Management; indeed, the first in the United Kingdom. He is also now head of the Department of Risk and Financial Services in the institution.

I wondered if people ever asked him how he has the time to work in the church and maintain a family life.

'Life is certainly very busy and hectic at times. I do travel a lot nationally and internationally and some people do ask me how I manage to juggle and keep all the balls in the air, as it were. I think, I would have to turn that question round and ask, "How on earth could I not be so involved in the church?" because I could not live for twenty-four hours a day without any other dimension to my life whatsoever. But, more importantly, without that Christian service dimension, would I simply wake up every morning and work until it was time to go to bed again? I know I could, as there is enough work to occupy me 36 hours a day!'

Gordon acknowledges that this is a dilemma which many face in their lives, but he also asserts that it is important to set priorities, nurturing each of the dimensions which matter to us, including family and church. Knowing how and when to unwind and relax, how to avoid the pressures of one affecting the other is important too. It is also necessary to be aware that interpersonal relations take place at a different level in each sphere of life.

'My daughter Julie, who is a university student at present, jokingly remarked, when I was talking about some of these dilemmas for this discussion, "Dilemmas? Dad, isn't your main dilemma whether to be nice or nasty to your undergraduates at a lecture on a Monday morning?"

'To take a serious point from this, I am aware that my students may well be influenced by what I say and do, just as my own family are, and do my best to reach out to the young folk in college, seeing them not as faceless undergraduates but people challenged by all that confronted me at that age - and more perhaps.

'It would be so easy to think of students in this way while neglecting my own family. We read a lot about the breakdown of family life today and I like to think that I value mine too much to allow that to happen. I am away from home more than many fathers but I try to make time whenever possible to relax, have holidays and be a friend as much as a parent to my daughters. There is also the danger, particularly at the teenage stage, that home becomes like a "Bed and Breakfast" establishment, without time being made for communication and sharing together outside these hours.

'While the "generation gap" is a fact of life, it need not destroy friendships and relationships within a family. It would be the easiest side to neglect and it is vital to be involved with your growing children before it is too late. At the same time, we must foster their independence, acknowledging that they are only ours for a short time. As many parents now admit, the nest is empty sooner than you think it will be.'

Life in an educational institution is no less fraught with problems than in an office or on a factory floor. Moral behaviour, attitudes and the prevalence of bad language are all topics which come up from time to time to challenge most people. Professors do not find them any easier to deal with than plumbers! But as a Christian in his work, Gordon has frequently to seek wisdom to know when, indeed whether, to chide or make a comment, without appearing to take the moral highground or abuse his position of authority.

'At the same time, later on in an evening, I may regret not having intervened in some situations with a timely word. Again, one would never be silent in some situations if a response were always to be made to every word of bad language. But I find it especially difficult to tolerate repeated blasphemy in conversation; even more so, from those in extremely high places whom I meet, when comment may appear to be discourteous. Nevertheless, I have found that disapproval can be shown in more subtle ways; by not responding, by not laughing nor smiling and perhaps changing the subject abruptly.'

Much of Gordon's international reputation is the result of his prolific writing on many topics within his field of Risk Management. He has written many articles, papers and textbooks and a number of the six current major titles he has been involved in publishing are key texts for courses throughout the world.

'I do appreciate the opportunity to write and contribute some of my knowledge and experience for the benefit of others. Writing does not come easy - *enjoy* would be the wrong word to use; *childbirth* would be more accurate - but I do get a sense of achievement when a book actually comes off the press. They are very specialist in content, however, and I am unlikely ever to hit the best-seller list in your High Street bookshop, nor to make my fortune, for that matter!'

Divinity, Mathematics, Education, Law etc. are all faculties we know about, but Risk Management certainly is not a subject most of us are familiar with. I asked Gordon to enlighten me on a subject discussed frequently by businesses throughout the world and important enough for a university professor to be appointed.

'I was once introduced at a meeting as a "Professor of Mismanagement", rather than Risk Management, which gave some of my colleagues a good laugh. My work involves teaching undergraduates and postgraduate supervision in addition to consultancy and industry liaison.

'Companies may ask for advice on measuring "risk" in their business and then request assistance in how to tackle and minimise it. They may have a large number of motor accidents, for example, and are unsure why this is taking place and what they can do to prevent them. We would then look at their accident records, analyse them, work out the trends and patterns and try to identify why they occur. Does it always happen at a particular time of day? Are particular drivers or types of vehicles involved? We might then recommend various physical means of controlling these.

'The same would apply to fire, theft etc. and some businesses may be finding that they can no longer afford to insure against those risks. A cost effective means of financing these risks may then be worked out. Solutions may be as simple as advising a company not to insure areas where there is very little risk involved and use the finance saved to improve other aspects of the business. Insurance may be the last step to take, if all other ways of reducing or financing the risk have been explored.'

One of the most bizarre cases he encountered involved a bus company who asked them to look at their loss record. It came to be known as 'The Black Widow Solution' for reasons which became clear as he explained.

'The company asked us to look at their loss record.

We discovered from their data that all was well when their drivers were travelling along on a straight road but, when pulling into stops, they kept hitting parked cars! We then had to work out a means of reducing that risk. Apart from "giant wiskers" or "rubber fenders" around the bumpers someone came up with the idea of "The Black Widow".

'They would recruit mainly older women who would join bus queues incognito, travel on the bus and get off. The hidden purpose, however, was to fill in a little form about the driver's traffic behaviour. Hence the title given to them by the wary drivers who found anonymous "spies in their cabs"!

'The work also involves writing manuals for companies, designing forms, training staff, etc. Much of my lecturing abroad is part of the training programme we offer to companies and other colleges. This generates finance for our consultancy as we charge fees to our clients.'

The subject in itself may seem pretty dry and boring to the majority of us and Gordon recognises that this may well seem to be the case to the casual observer. However, for him, apart from his acknowledged expertise, he enjoys the whole business of working with and for people.

'If we can prevent accidents and injuries or improve business to allow them to remain solvent and maintain employment, I find it to be most satisfying. As a Christian, the opportunity to meet people from all walks of life and from different backgrounds at home and abroad is also personally satisfying for me and, I trust, a contribution to the economic wellbeing of this and other countries. Fairness, honesty and equity in business are human, indeed Christian, qualities I value and trust I express in my dealings with others. So much of business and commercial life can be tainted that I believe that clients can notice the difference.

'The Bible gives no specific guidance on how to be a professor or how to deal with the subject of Risk Management. The life of Jesus does not show me what to do in these matters. But Christ certainly shows us how to deal with people and what our priorities should be in our personal and business life. It is a far deeper conviction and drive that determines what we do; it is not simply a matter of referring to a rule book. That to me is the key to witness in the world today.

'Meeting with, and lecturing to students is also satisfying and I value the opportunity to share my faith when young folk come to me. It may initially be on an academic matter they approach me but, from time to time, they come to confide in me with other, more personal, concerns. As in my work with mission teams, I find that people are more interested in who we are as individuals than in what we do and say. When one reflects the other, there is often a quest to find out more about the spiritual dimension to life.'

As already mentioned, his work involves considerable travel at home and abroad; less romantic and enjoyable than some might imagine, he stressed. But he does like to 'arrive', experience other cultures, meet other peoples and apply what he learns in other places.

'I enjoy aspects of this wider work and appreciate the opportunities afforded to me, but it can be lonely at times. Hotel rooms and airports are much the same all over the world but, when I do visit nice places I miss the opportunity to share my experience with my friends and family. Recalling personal adventures can be a bit of a bore for those who are left behind, so I do not relish long spells away from my family. This was brought home to me particularly when, on one occasion, I attended church when I had to spend several weekends abroad. Singing familiar hymns can be very poignant and make me homesick, bringing a tear to my eye, I am not afraid to confess.'

As illustrated by his experience in Nairobi, international travel can also have its adventures. This is only one of many he told me about. Apart from missing luggage, he has had his case rifled and been threatened by gun toting security guards. Some encounters can be deceiving, however, as he recounted.

'I recall arriving in Auckland, New Zealand. I was first off the plane and therefore at the beginning of the queue at Immigration Control. From the back of this ever growing snake it would have appeared that I was being closely interrogated by an officer, slowly leafing through my passport. Perhaps they thought I was some illegal immigrant, spy or smuggler. In fact, the man had emigrated from my home area twenty years before. He simply wanted to talk about his former town and country and the progress of his favourite football team! I reluctantly obliged by engaging him in conversation, not sure whether it was my place to say that there was a very large queue of irate passengers behind me!

'Less humorous was the occasion when I opened my case in Melbourne, having had a stop-over in Hong Kong to find that the contents had been rifled. While there was nothing missing, I recalled the experience of others who were caught up in a smuggling incident when, unknown to them, their case was used to carry drugs into a country. It was a useful Risk Management lesson to me as I now see the importance of the plastic tape which they weld on to cases on international journeys.'

From time to time there is also the opportunity to attend church abroad and Gordon finds that this rarely fails to have an impact on him.

'I have happy memories of warm fellowship offered to me, giving me a sense of home from home in some congregations. I was particularly aware of this during a six month spell in the United States, even although I had my family with me then. On the other hand, I recall churches whose members were cold and unwelcoming, often on occasions when I was alone and would have valued an outstretched hand in greeting or an invitation to meet and talk. This is a lesson I have not forgotten when I see a stranger in my own church.'

When I invited Gordon Dickson to tell me about his work, he considered that his life and career were not controversial enough nor fraught with the dilemmas faced in some other professions. The story which un-folded, however, highlighted how he has put his gifts, of communication and the ability to relate well with others, to good use, not only in his secular life but also in his work within the context of the church. His faith and personal commitment to Christ permeate all aspects of his life.

When we examine the Gospels and consider the life of Jesus and his disciples, that is surely what it is all about. Believers in the early church took a great risk in standing up for what they believed. It may be easier in certain respects today, but some might still view such personal commitment as a 'risky business'. After all, it may still involve one's standing out from the crowd, often professing belief in things which cannot be seen.

Gordon Dickson would argue that faith is the vital ingredient which removes that uncertainty and he is in no doubt that living in this way is certainly a risk worth taking.

7
Flying Solo

It was a beautiful day for flying: a bright blue sky was broken only by the occasional cloud. The cadet pilot had successfully carried out the required sequence of manoeuvres for her final test flight of the series. 'You have control, Miss Guilliard,' the flying instructor announced, calmly.

'I have control,' she replied, as she checked her instruments and awaited further directions.

The words had scarcely left her lips when, suddenly and without warning, the plane began to lose height rapidly and took a nosedive. She instinctively put into practice all that she had learned during her training but, as she pulled up, her heart racing, the blood drained from her head and everything turned black.

'I can't see! I can't see!' she cried out desperately.

She had just experienced what every pilot dreads - 'grey-out'- the term used when the force of gravity - the G force - causes blood to drain from the head, resulting first of all in tunnel vision and then a moment when everything turns grey. If the pull out continues at speed, total loss of vision and black-out ensues.

To her dismay, there was no response from her copilot. Had he blacked out too? For a fleeting moment she thought she might die as the plane continued to descend rapidly.

'Why doesn't he say something? Why doesn't he do something?'

The questions raced around in her head as she wrestled to regain control ... if only she could see the instruments; see where she was going. But, such was the force of gravity that she could not even lift her arms to reach forward from her seat.

Somehow, she managed to recover the plane. Her heart was still thumping when the instructor remarked casually, 'Well done, Miss Guilliard, you pulled four and a half G there. You got out of that one beautifully. I wondered how you would react when I did that to you.'

Although Jane wanted to say a lot more, perhaps even to give him a piece of her mind for putting her through such an emergency procedure without warning, she replied simply, 'Thank you, Sir.' and flew on as if nothing had happened.

She knew that soon she would be flying solo, with no instructor to guide or praise and that emergencies at several thousand feet at great speed were just that - emergencies. During her training to become a pilot with British Airways, she had come to expect a thorough and detailed assessment of her ability from her unpredictable colleague, a former pilot with a daredevil aerobatic team. She should have guessed that he would try her to the limit on one of the major final tests before qualifying.

Jane Guilliard, still only in her early twenties, told me the story of her life to date. It became clear that she has been 'flying solo', in more ways than one, for a large part of her life. For many years she has had a single-minded determination to defy those who tried to divert her to 'more feminine' occupations and, during many frustrating years of education to achieve her professional goals, she has doggedly maintained her Christian faith and witness.

Many hours of examinations and exhausting periods of training among a group of men, not all sympathetic to her beliefs, tested her patience and faith to the limit.

Born in the attractive Channel Island of Jersey, Jane is one of few women to succeed in being chosen to train as a pilot with a major world airline. Her achievement did not surprise her parents, for they remember how the first suggestion came when she was in primary school. The notion developed into an obsession and soon became an unwavering determination. Jane recalled those early days when she was attending a girls' school on the island.

'As a child I was very interested in mechanical things, construction toys and the like. I much preferred to play with Lego or try to repair things than to sew, knit or cook, the usual pastimes towards which many girls are steered. But it was more than that, as I remember.

'When I was about eight years old, one of my teachers was taking us through a project on Flight - still a popular theme in primary schools today. I was fascinated by the topic and even more so when the RAF father of my teacher came to speak to us. He talked about planes and navigation using terms such as, *tail winds, head winds* and so on, all to tie in with the work we had been doing, which included the study of birds and man's first attempts at flying. Unlike some of the other girls, I was engrossed and took it all in.'

That evening she returned home and announced to her parents that she wanted to be a pilot when she grew up. They did not take her too seriously as, like most girls of her age, she had already talked about doing other things. More to have something to say than to discourage their daughter out of hand, they pointed out that it was difficult to become a pilot and that it was likely to cost more than they could afford to allow her to train. Just as her wish on earlier occasions to be a nurse, doctor or policewoman, this would surely go away.

Trips to the local airport and frequent holiday flights abroad, when she was often found on the flight deck, only served to fuel her obsession. By the time she left primary school her mind was set. But other things were to occupy her mind at that time also.

Brought up in a Christian home, she regularly attended the local Baptist Church with her parents, was a member of the Sunday School and, in her teens, became involved with Christian Endeavour. By the time she moved to secondary school she was already very familiar with the Bible and many aspects of Christian living. Concurrent, therefore, with her professional ambition was her growing interest in spiritual things.

'I cannot remember a time when I was not taught to trust the Word of God for direction in my life. I recall, when I was about fifteen, hearing some wonderful testimonies of how individuals had had dramatic conversion experiences and I wondered if there was something wrong with me. I knew about right and wrong, I knew about sin and salvation - all the correct terminology - but Christ had come into my life quietly and simply as I got to know about him.

'Yes, there was a juncture in my life when I made a public confession of faith; this was at the age of 17 when I was baptised. But it was from my mother's knee, I learned about Jesus Christ and the Good News which he brought. I was soon familiar with all of the Bible stories and, in a home atmosphere which I now recognise as being very stable and sheltered, I was carefully nurtured in a faith which I came to rely on in later years.

'Nearly all of my friends went to church and my parents must have been pleased when, apart from the occasional tantrum, I did not go through the traumatic teenage years that some do. I think I was too busy with church activities or enjoying sport and recreation with my friends; or perhaps it was the preoccupation with my goal to become a pilot and the related studying I had to do.

'I knew about prayer and soon found myself, selfishly perhaps, asking God to help me to succeed in what I wanted to do. I remember being amused when the verse given to me when I was received into church membership was, *They shall mount up with wings of eagles. They shall run and not be weary. They shall walk and not faint.* This was a most appropriate verse for me as you will understand when I tell you more.

'My prayers were answered but not until God had taught me so many things along the way, including such things as patience and endurance; qualities I lacked at times in my youth.'

In secondary school Jane already had a list of subjects which she had to pass to be accepted for training as a cadet. She passed the first hurdle of 'O' levels and proceeded to select her 'A' level subjects; these had to be physics, geography and mathematics. To her great surprise and disappointment, she learned that she would not be able to study physics. The other subjects would be possible but, reflecting attitudes in these days, physics was only available in the boys' school!

'That was the first major attempt to divert me from what I wanted to do. They brought up all sorts of reasons why it would not be wise to take the subject, including my low passmark at 'O' level. In fact, looking back now, they said everything but, 'Why on earth do you want to be a pilot anyway?' Nevertheless, I still remained adamant and refused to heed a single piece of advice.'

To more than a few remarks from her friends, Jane transferred to the boys' school to a class where she was the only girl. She survived, 'flying solo' and, against the odds, succeeded in obtaining a pass in physics.

As an added bonus, she met Martin Delap (coincidentally, good at physics!) to whom she is now engaged to be married. However, she had worked so hard in science that she had neglected her studies in geography and maths. She marginally failed them.

To add to her dilemma at this time, her mother was diagnosed as having cancer and there followed a period of distress and uncertainty. As an only child, born to her parents when they were in their forties, she did not wish to consider the prospect of leaving Jersey to pursue her career if her mother's health were to deteriorate further.

'It was a very difficult period for the whole family and we had to trust in God one day at a time. You can understand how hard it was to contemplate my future during these months.'

Thankfully, her mother made a remarkable recovery and was keen for Jane to continue with her education. Prior to sitting her exams, she applied to British Airways when she saw an advert for a training programme for cadet pilots. Despite the setback with her results she was called to London to sit entrance exams. Several tests, including logic, hand-eye co-ordination and a rather difficult series on mathematics were presented to her. She was informed that she had passed all but one, which she assumed to be the paper on logic. Heartbroken, she returned home, believing that God did not seem to be answering her prayers.

'I was to learn over the next few years that, on each occasion when a door closed in my face, another would open. I didn't think of it as God's guidance in those days; it seemed more of an impediment to my progress and an utter waste of my time than a part of some plan for my life. I consider now that what happened to me was very much part of a plan God had for me; to become a pilot but, above all, to lead me to maturity in my Christian life.'

A wise, equally determined, careers teacher had previously insisted that she should widen her horizons. She managed to persuade her to apply to the Civil Aviation Authority to become an air traffic controller. Also a relatively unique occupation for women, it would fulfil her ambition to be involved with planes; a second best perhaps, but a reasonable alternative, given her interests and qualifications.

She succeeded in passing geography and began

training with the CAA in Bournemouth on a course which, in addition to the anticipated subjects related to air traffic control, she learned that she would have to attend an Outward Bound induction course in the Lake District.

'Work as an air traffic controller demands close co-operation with colleagues in all situations, during emergencies and in times of stress. The Outward Bound course was as much an opportunity for our instructors to observe how we related to each other in challenging situations as it was for us to learn how to get on with each other and to co-operate to achieve given goals.

'I hate camping; hate being outdoors in all weathers, so this was quite a trial for me. I needed to pray for lots of patience and endurance, not least because I was among so many hardy, macho men who seemed to take it all in their stride. At the same time I was determined not to give even a hint that I couldn't cope or indicate that the going was too rough for me!'

As expected, she was one of only two girls on the course which was being followed by men of a wide age range and from a variety of backgrounds. The lonely experience in the boys' school proved to have been a good grounding for her.

'The boys at secondary school soon found that I was more than a match for them and I would not allow them to take advantage of me - in all respects! Although I learned then to stand up for myself as a girl in a crowd of boys, it was more difficult for me as a woman in a world of men on the induction course.

'When you are one of few females in a group it is interesting to observe how other people judge you.

They either think that you will be highly macho or extrovertly feminine. I just wanted to be myself, without compromising my gender, and underline that I was, in all other respects, "one of the boys" as far as the organisers were concerned. I did not wish to be given any privileges nor to be exempt from the more rigorous parts of the course.'

After Jane had established these principles, the majority of the men accepted her for who she was. Once she had made an initial witness to her Christian beliefs, while it was not all plain sailing, the majority respected the position she also held in this regard.

Having been brought up in the sheltered atmosphere of a Christian home, it was a bit of a culture shock for Jane to meet men with such a contrasting attitude to life and their total lack of knowledge of many basic things in the Bible.

'I had lived a life which centred on the church and Christian things. Perhaps naively, I had taken it all for granted and accepted it as the norm. It was quite something for me to meet people who had decided that they did not believe in God and who were not interested at all in Christian things. While there were occasions when they would ask why I wouldn't do this or that, talking about it seemed futile. I felt that I had to live out my faith by showing them who I was and what I stood for, without getting on to a soap box or appearing to be "holier than thou".

'I realise now that, had my faith not been so strong and firmly established, the whole experience might have been an overwhelming temptation to taste and see what their world had to offer. I now believe that God was preparing me for many more challenges in the years ahead.'

The course proved to be more rigorous than anticipated and there was a high percentage dropout rate. Jane was one of only seven to graduate out of eighteen.

'I did not feel that I was the "token female" accepted by the CAA to keep on the right side of the Sex Discrimination Act, but I was always conscious that I was in the minority. I was pleased to do so well in such a competitive cohort of highly motivated and well educated male cadets.'

During her training she had to become familiar with various air traffic control units throughout the country. Her first posting was to Glasgow, a city she knew little about in a country she had not visited before.

'My parents, who had never been to Scotland, were quite shocked that I had chosen to go so far from home. During my five weeks there I had a wonderful time and received such a warm welcome from the controllers - and not just because I was the only female!'

To her delight she learned that she would have to do fifteen hours of flying training to familiarise her with various procedures which pilots had to undertake and to appreciate what it is like to be 'on the receiving end' of air traffic control. This short experience only served to whet her appetite. She was determined to fly again, even if only as a hobby.

After further training on a control simulator she was posted to Manchester where she appreciated the friendships she made there in her work and in the church she attended. Flying remained her ambition but she was soon caught up in the interesting work in which she was engaged. She enjoyed the challenge presented to her by the responsibility of the job; the tension of the watch when an airport is busy with planes stacking, holding, landing and, taxiing. Once again, she was the only female controller.

'I came to realise that, despite the seriousness of the work, a sense of humour was essential to relax us and relieve the occasional tense moments. It was always a good laugh for my colleagues when pilots called me *sir* over the air, invariably correcting it with, "er, I mean, er, m'am".

'I also recall listening to the pilot of a large American transatlantic jet taxiing out. When he saw a much smaller British Airways turbo prop on the ground, he asked, "Hey, BA what do you call that little thing down there?" The BA response was sharp and indignant, "This is a British Aerospace Advanced Turbo-prop, I will have you know!" "Really?" came the reply from the jet, "Did you make it yourself?"

'On another occasion we had a good laugh when a pilot transmitted his announcement, "Ladies and gentlemen, welcome aboard this 747 flight to Chicago..." without realising that he was still switched to air traffic control and not to the passengers in the cabin behind him!'

As the course progressed, they were informed one day that, to meet immediate requirements for controllers in the CAA, they would have to specialise in training for 'area' control. This implied that they would mainly be training to deal with larger, higher planes and would inevitably find themselves with little choice of postings.

'The main work in this sector was either in the

Scottish centre at Prestwick or the London centre in West Drayton. It was quite a blow for me to learn, at the age of twenty, that I would have little choice in where I would be posted to continue with my career. I remember sharing it with my folks at home and praying a lot about it when I came across a British Airways advertisement for pilots. I applied and, to my surprise, got a quick reply informing me that, as I had only failed one of the tests last time round, I need only do that part again.'

In the meantime, she continued with the area controllers' course, appreciating the experience in simulation and radar which she was given. She was then compulsorily posted to London just before an interview and test with BA.

'Unsure now of my future with the CAA, I swotted up on Logic, the exam I reckoned I had failed last time with British Airways. Logic was coming out of my ears when I arrived to take the test. "Miss Guilliard, you only have to take the Maths mental arithmetic test, so we can get on with that and let you go." I was more than a little stunned, and was terrified I would fail.'

But she passed, and a call to a final interview held out the prospect of her ambition being fulfilled at last. Her training in air traffic control stood her in good stead and gave her the edge over many other applicants. The knowledge and experience gained would be of assistance to her as a potential pilot. She learned that three hundred had been selected from almost fifteen thousand applicants. Jane was one of twenty girls chosen to start training that year.

'The CAA were not too pleased when I resigned as soon as I graduated, but I was over the moon to be accepted to train as an airline pilot and without any expense to myself or my parents. Unlike many other companies, British Airways did not ask for any contribution towards the average training cost of £80,000.'

Having survived the challenge of her schooling with the CAA and coped with the need to train alongside people, not initially sympathetic to her beliefs, she now found herself back to square one, to all intents and purposes. She was 'flying solo' yet again.

'I found myself the sole female again among a bunch of guys more young and immature than I imagined BA cadets would be. My experience with air traffic control now seemed very much in God's plan for me. Parts of the course content were similar and I tackled them with much more confidence than I would have done several years before. This meant that I had more time to concentrate on the areas in which I required further knowledge and with greater determination to meet the challenge of working with some of the men.

'Often I had to contend with smutty jokes and insinuating remarks, which not all of the women around us objected to. I found it more difficult to deal with when it came from an instructor but, on most occasions, they soon gave up if I did not react to them. They also became aware of my moral principles; that I did not go out with all and sundry or sleep around. It did not occur to me that they would take note when I didn't go home to my boyfriend's flat overnight from time to time, as seemed to be the thing to do.

'I was encouraged to learn that a number of the ground instructors were Christians and it was at that time I heard about the Airline, Aviation and Aerospace

Christian Fellowship. The Association organises events for staff in all of the major airports and aviation centres in the United Kingdom.'

Her delight was tempered with dismay when she found herself allocated again to attend an Outward Bound course, this time in the Scottish Highlands!

'I think God wanted to try me! There was I, loathing all things to do with the outdoors, thrown among a group of men, to rough it and try to survive against the elements.'

The beauty of the setting did little to endear her to the experience which turned out to be ten times more arduous than the adventure planned by the CAA. But, if she were to achieve that elusive goal, she simply had to keep silent, grin and bear it.

'If ever I needed God's help it was then. I found myself in a cold, wet environment in the middle of February, forced to share a tent with one of the men. We set off and I suffered it with the minimum of complaint, but the fellow was well warned not to cross the dividing line I had created in the close quarters of the canvas, even although part of the training was to learn to survive by "sharing each other's body heat". "I'm cold and I want a cuddle," my partner protested. Fortunately, I had known him for a couple of years and we had a good laugh about our predicament.'

To keep her spirits up she imagined that she was basking in the sun of a tropical island rather than enduring a windy winter night, high on a Scottish hillside, with the temperature dropping. She tried to convince herself that the noise of the water lapping on the shores of the loch was the sound of surf on golden sand. In reality, she was cold, exhausted and scared that she would roll towards her companion for warmth as she slept and would wake up in his arms!

She survived the ordeal and was greatly relieved when, as if in reward for her endurance, she was posted to more luxurious accommodation at a base in Prestwick. Once more away from home she was unsure what she would find there. During her sixteen months training on basic flying principles, the programme was so intense that many of her fellow cadets studied into the small hours, perhaps with the occasional binge at a party on a weekend off, followed by long sleeps to catch up for lost time. Again, the temptation might have been for her to go along with the crowd, be one of them and similarly unwind.

Jane took an early opportunity to show that this was not the way she led her life and set off on the first available Sunday to find a church and fellowship to occupy some of her free time in Prestwick. The local Baptist Church welcomed her and many families opened their homes to her for meals and friendship during her stay. She soon got involved in church activities when she was free, particularly when they learned that she could sing. This turned out to be a ministry which the church appreciated. There were also many opportunities to witness and give testimony to her faith.

'The group soon realised that I was not around on a Sunday. They knew I was often asked out for meals by the friends I met there and, as the food wasn't very good on the course, they would joke with me that I went to church just to get one good meal a week. I did appreciate the lovely meals I had but it was not easy for them to accept that it was spiritual food I was after also! Eight months into the course I was delighted when a cadet from Northern Ireland, a committed Christian, came to train with another group. He was very pleased to be able to come to church with me as I had a car and could give him a lift. It was also great to be able to talk to him from time to time.

'The course was rigorous, and at times depressing. For a period of about eight weeks I rarely saw daylight. The opportunity to have fellowship in a welcoming church helped sustain me, body, mind and spirit. In contrast, some others on the course were not able to relax away from the training. I think some thought I was a bit odd when I didn't "let my hair down" in their way, but I have a sneaking suspicion that a few of them envied me.'

The real flying soon began and she was pleased to have a sympathetic and patient instructor who neither patronised her for being a woman nor made any exceptions to her gender. Training took her on flights all over Scotland. But the same landscape, with its attractive mountains and glens also presents pilots with hazards to contend with such as electricity pylons and unpredictable weather.

Ground school, to learn about aerodynamics, principles of flight, navigation, flight instrumentation, radio theory etc. continued on alternate days: this all led to technical exams.

'I enjoyed that part of the course and realised it was essential, but I could not wait to get off the ground on the other days. I had to ensure that I paid as much attention to the theory as to the practical since there was a very high pass mark. Some of the guys who seemed to be doing well were put out of the course, so you can imagine how stunned I was when I learned that, with 65%, I was in danger of following them.'

She was disappointed to be told that she had not reached the required standard in one area of work. To her relief, she was allowed to resit - but there was a drawback. She had to resit all the exams and had to join a new group to do additional training.

'Having put so much time and effort into the training, I was very annoyed and depressed and might have given up in disgust; but not quite! I pulled myself together and saw it as just one more hurdle on the track I had ventured onto. With all the determination I could muster and lots of faith and strength from God, I said to myself, "I'll show them. They won't get rid of me so easily!"

'It all turned out well in the end. I found myself finishing my training with a much more pleasant, helpful and sympathetic group of men. Without doubt, this helped me to relax much more than I might have done with some of the guys I had met before. Perhaps it was all in God's plan yet again, not only to help me pass the course, but also to learn a little more patience.'

Flight training on the Swiss-made Bravo included aerobatics, the prospect of which she dreaded and thought might cause her to pull back from her ambition.

Jane was a bit surprised that such manoeuvres were part of the training as it is not the sort of thing the average transatlantic or domestic pilot is called to do to the passengers! But she learned that they were to give an appreciation of spatial awareness following an incident when a 747 jet hit severe turbulence over the Pacific and turned completely upside down. The pilot, who had done some aerobatics, carried out the correct procedures and righted the plane by referring to his instruments, without causing it to break up. Learning to read instruments in all sorts of positions is now an essential part of the training with British Airways.

'I prayed for a good instructor who would take my fears and dread of being sick into account. I was not disappointed. In fact, he turned out to be my previous instructor and he helped me a lot by confessing that, as a RAF pilot, he used to hate it also and was sick on more than one occasion. "If you don't like it, we'll stop," he reassured me. I got through it and had to learn a sequence of aerobatics for my final exam. I didn't enjoy it exactly but neither was I gripped with the fear I once had.'

Accurate navigation, even in extreme ground weather conditions, is essential for pilots and this was also a hazardous and trying part of the training. On one occasion she was flying a Warrior in the Scottish mountains on a navigation test, with deep snow on the ground, when she was asked to locate a particular landmark on the map.

'Imagine my surprise when I was told in the end that it was a phone box! Although it should have been red, it was invisible in the snow. I had to locate it by a precise navigation technique. No instruments were used; only a clock to allow me to calculate the location by the flight time from the starting position. I found it for him and felt quite pleased with myself.'

One hundred and fifty flying hours later she found herself on that all so important flight when she experienced 'grey-out'. I wondered if in both real and simulated emergencies like that she ever found herself praying, to herself, or even out loud.

'Many people might think of prayer as a lengthy and deliberate act of supplication. When fear strikes or emergencies occur, I do find that I am in fact praying but it is so instant and urgent on these occasions that it is little more than "HELP". I suppose that is no less of a prayer to God's ears than a more long-winded one. I am not ashamed to say that I pray - perhaps not as frequently as I should - but I have often been conscious of God's presence in many situations in my life.

'Fear and panic were not in the book as far as my training was concerned, only positive reactions to the unforeseen! But I do recall on one occasion becoming slightly disorientated when I flew unexpectedly into dark clouds on a solo navigational exercise. But I did not panic. Prayer in that situation was, "Lord help me to remember what I was trained to do." I remembered the procedures and got out of the clouds to return to base without any difficulty.

'It may be of interest to some of my future passengers to know that I am a Christian and that I pray about my work, but I am certain that most would be more reassured to learn that I have been highly trained to deal with many of the emergencies that can occur. This does not mean that I consider prayer as a last resort but, as with most professions, frequently we must use the skills and knowledge which God has allowed us to have, to get out of tricky spots in life.'

Jane is ever conscious of the responsibility involved in being a pilot and identifies with every emergency situation she hears about or reads in the newspapers. She particularly recalls hearing about the British Midland crash at East Midlands airport as she knew the pilot of the plane.

'In my teenage days of obsession with all things to do with flying, I couldn't keep away from airports. I had a summer job with British Midland as a load controller when I met him. He was one of the first people to show a genuine interest in my ambition to fly and talked to me about what I needed to do to be accepted for training. Although pleased to learn that he had survived I was sorry to know that he was confined to a wheelchair. I wrote to him to tell him what I was now doing and referred to his encouraging advice. I got a delightful reply from him.

'People often ask me how I cope with the risks and hazards associated with flying but I have to point out that, statistically, driving, or even being a pedestrian, are much more dangerous. Wherever we are, whatever we are doing, we have to trust in God and the skills of other people for our safety.'

Her written finals included sitting twenty-two exams in three days, with a pass mark of over 70%, to obtain that much sought-after licence. Only a limited number of resits were allowed in any of the small sections which were assessed. This intensity continued over a period of several months during her time at college; a feat of endurance in itself but very much part of the test to find out how she could work under pressure. There were, of course, many medical examinations and questionnaires to cope with also.

'It was all quite nerve-wracking and exhausting. It

was also frustrating, as I did have to resit for some areas of work. Among the hardest was climatology as it is essential to be familiar with the weather in all parts of the world at different times of the year.'

Her flying continued, this time in a twin-engined Piper Seneca, six seater, to learn about instrument flying and, most importantly, engine failure.

'We spent most of our early training in single engine planes and longed to fly a twin engined aircraft, only to discover that they kept shutting one of them down when we did. But I really enjoyed that time as I felt it was a major step towards 'real flying' as far as the airline was concerned. We also were able to fly all over the country in training exercises and have the opportunity to have a "land away" as a bonus after the instrument rating test. I surprised my parents one day when we dropped into Jersey for a lunch break from Prestwick.'

Simulator jet training followed, with more sophisticated instruments and procedures as well as simulated flights with "passengers" with whom she would communicate during the flight. Added to this there was training on emergency landings, "bomb scares" and many other emergency situations which can arise at any time in the life of a pilot. Jane could now set her sights on the last hurdle before qualification; her final flight test.

Then it was graduation at last; delight and relief to her and her parents. Once sceptical of her flight of fancy, they had, nevertheless, supported her through the years of success and the tears of failure. They had much to be thankful for but, above all, they were grateful that their prayers had been answered. Not only had she succeeded in making her dream become reality, but she had also been a witness to the faith she had been led to by their prayers and example.

The ambition of every trainee pilot is to fly solo. Jane had done that on many occasions, but they and she knew that, as far as God was concerned with her life, there was no time when she was ever really alone.

One of these days, when you are jetting off on holiday, don't be too taken aback if you hear a female voice announcing over the intercom, 'Good evening ladies and gentlemen, this is your captain speaking ...' It may well be Jane Guilliard at the controls.